"The world was peopled
with wonders."

The origin of Wildsam comes from above, a
line of prose in the novel *East of Eden,* written by
John Steinbeck. Six words hinting at a broad and
interwoven idea. One of curiosity, connection, joy. And
the belief that stories have the power to unearth the
mysteries of a place—for anyone. The book in
your hands is rooted in such things.

Deep thanks to those who provided Seattle-style navigational wisdom as we explored this great city: the Duwamish Tribe and Cecile Hansen; Abby Cerquitella and *Spilled Milk*; Timothy White Eagle; the archives of the Seattle Public Library, City of Seattle and University of Washington; Colin Camacho at Filson; Mark Canlis; Amie Henson; *The Seattle Times*; Kiliii Yuyan; Bob Forgrave at Cascade Orienteering Club; Jourdan Imani Keith; and Charles D'Ambrosio. We are grateful to the city's frontline health workers, top-notch researchers and first responders, who dealt with a pandemic as we were researching this book.

WILDSAM FIELD GUIDES™

Copyright © 2020

Published in the United States by Wildsam Field Guides, Austin, Texas.

ISBN 978-1-4671-9908-7

Illustrations by Jordan Kay

To find more field guides, please visit www.wildsam.com

CONTENTS

*Discover the people and places
that tell the story of Seattle*

WELCOME

EDWARD CARLSON BELIEVED his city needed something. Big, sure, but definitely bold. Carlson hustled his way up in Seattle, from bellhop to hotel executive. Come the late 1950s, he was leading Seattle's plans to host a world's fair, a chance for a city considered somewhat remote [not to mention soggy] to audition on a global stage. Carlson pulled out a napkin one day and started sketching. His doodle gave birth to the Space Needle, Seattle's jaunty beacon.

You can read the Needle many ways, from *Jetsons* kitsch to high-tech shrine. To us, it reveals one of Seattle's under-appreciated qualities: sheer, brassy ambition. One early pioneer settlement here dubbed itself "New York Alki"—*alki* being Chinook for "someday." Since then, an outsider, beat-the-world drive has powered the city's journey. The Northwest historian Stewart Holbrook observed, "Seattle is a place of singleness of mind. The idea is always a Bigger and Better Seattle." He meant that as a dig. We read it as a compliment.

Out in the Far Corner, ringed with water, Seattle is a destined gateway. A "crossing-over place" for the Indigenous peoples before colonialism. The staging ground for Klondike prospectors in sepia-toned days. [Johnny Horton's rallying cry: *"Big Sam left Seattle in the year of '92 …"*] A hinge between the West and the Pacific world.

This setting seems to inspire dreams of transformation. In 50 years, Boeing went from building wooden seaplanes to 747s. Here, a Brooklyn-born sales guy imagined an espresso bar on every corner—and made it happen. Kurt Cobain, disgruntled guitarist from a logging town, came here to give grunge the pop touch it needed to go big. More recently, the poet Claudia Castro Luna set out to map Seattle in verse, inviting writers from all neighborhoods to reimagine the city as a "poetic grid." Ambition takes many forms and serves many ends.

The city has surged in recent boom times. But the past abides here, too. An easy walk links South Lake Union's futuristic glass domes to Pioneer Square's mossy brick. That history contains its own ugliness: Native displacement, anti-Chinese riots, Japanese internment, the redlining of Black neighborhoods. And it sometimes also reveals a city meeting its moment, worthy of its aspirations, sketching what comes next. —The Editors

ESSENTIALS

TRANSPORT

SEAPLANE
Kenmore Air
kenmoreair.com

....

FERRIES
Washington State Ferries
wsdot.wa.gov

....

KAYAK
Alki Kayak Tours
kayakalki.com

LANDMARKS

MOPOP
325 Fifth Ave N
A wild eruption of Frank Gehry design houses a trove of pop culture artifacts.

....

A SOUND GARDEN
7600 Sand Point Way NE
Douglas Hollis' sonic sculpture inspired the band name.

MEDIA

NEWS
The Stranger
Take-no-prisoners news and culture: an alt-alt weekly.

....

Seattle Metropolitan
Glossy, literate city deep dive.

....

AUDIO
KEXP 90.3 FM
The definitive indie station.

GREENSPACE

DISCOVERY PARK
3801 Discovery Park Blvd
Semi-wild ex-fort commands mountain and Sound views.

....

WASHINGTON PARK ARBORETUM
1300 Arboretum Dr E
An ark of native plants and international biomes.

....

VOLUNTEER PARK
1247 15th Ave E
Olmsted-designed classic, featuring a soaring conservatory.

CALENDAR

JAN - MAY
Seattle Chamber Music Fest
Emerald City Comicon
Mariners & Sounders

MAY - JUL
International Film Fest
Seattle Pride
Capitol Hill Block Party

AUG - DEC
Seafair
Hempfest
Bumbershoot
Earshot Jazz

BOOKS

☞ *Skid Road*
  by Murray Morgan
☞ *Where'd You Go, Bernadette*
  by Maria Semple
☞ *No-No Boy* by John Okada

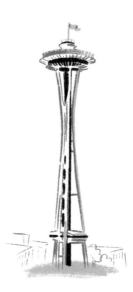

MEMENTOS

Sea salt dark chocolate bar, *Theo Chocolate*, $4
Tin Cloth cruiser jacket, *Filson*, $350
White Shino stoneware mug, *Natasha Alphonse Studio Ceramics*, $62

RECORD COLLECTION

The Sonics	*!!!Here Are the Sonics!!!*
Brandi Carlile	*The Firewatcher's Daughter*
Mudhoney	*Superfuzz Bigmuff*
Shabazz Palaces	*Black Up*
Nirvana	*Nevermind*
Sir Mix-A-Lot	*Swass*
The Gits	*Frenching the Bully*
Pearl Jam	*Ten*
Guayaba	*Fantasmagoría*
Soundgarden	*Louder Than Love*
La Luz	*Weirdo Shrine*
Fleet Foxes	*Sun Giant*
Blue Scholars	*Blue Scholars*
Tacocat	*Lost Time*

ESSENTIALS

LODGING

Hotel Sorrento
900 Madison St
1909-built aristocrat fit for Nick and Nora. Dunbar Room martini, please.

....

Ace Hotel
2423 1st Ave
Pace-setting brand's original outpost: an oddly perfect austere-cozy balance.

....

Palihotel
107 Pine St
Retro-nautical charm pairs with warm service, right by Pike Place Market.

The Arctic Club
700 3rd Ave
Founded by Klondike gold rush magnates, with matching manly throwback vibes.

....

Hotel Ballard
5216 Ballard Ave NW
A plush spread in the thick of Ballard, at heart a Scandinavian fishing village.

....

Capt. Whidbey Inn
Whidbey Island
Ferry-hop to a way-back lodge and fancy-rustic cabins. You're the captain now.

WELLNESS

Métier
The fanciest of cycling clubhouses, with rentals and rides, both social and "club pace." *1017 E Union St, Capitol Hill*

....

Stone Gardens
Sprawling indoor climbing gym. Wicked angles in "the Realm." *1839 NW Market St, Ballard*

....

8 Limbs
Four locations and a socially inclusive message, exploring meaning as well as movement—a very Seattle yoga approach. *8limbsyoga.com*

ART GALLERIES

Frye Art Museum
704 Terry Ave
First Hill

....

Greg Kucera
212 3rd Ave S
Pioneer Square

....

Henry Art Gallery
University of Washington

BOOKSTORES

Elliott Bay
Capitol Hill
The city's literary base camp.

....

Peter Miller
Downtown
Architecture and design buff pilgrimage.

....

L.E.M.S. Life Enrichment
Columbia City
Black-owned staple for events.

....

Magus Books
University District
Magical, ivy-clad nook for new, used and rare.

ISSUES

Earthquakes	It's a matter of *when* not *if* the Cascadia subduction zone will generate a quake up to magnitude 9, potentially killing and displacing thousands and causing a tsunami that could reach as far as Japan. Preparation is a constant topic. **EXPERT:** *Erin Wirth, University of Washington/U.S. Geological Survey*
Housing	HUD ranks Seattle/King County's housing crisis the third worst in the country. Thousands are experiencing some form of homelessness, and many lack access to any shelter at all. Historic redlining and current gentrification shape equity and demographics. **EXPERT:** *Rex Hohlbein, Facing Homelessness*
Transportation	Seattle has the nation's seventh-worst congestion, with commuters stuck an average of 78 hours a year, per the 2019 Urban Mobility Report. Clashing viewpoints—more roads versus more robust public transit—extend the crisis. **EXPERT:** *Mark Hallenbeck, Washington State Transportation Center*
Coronavirus	The first U.S. region to report COVID-19 cases had an unfortunate head start on calamity—and an early edge in countering the outbreak, along with lessons for the next pandemic. **EXPERT:** *Keith Jerome, University of Washington Virology Lab*

STATISTICS

53,500	Amazon employees in region
14%	Odds a megaquake hits the city, next 50 years
80	Days in year Mount Rainier visible [approx.]
122,000	Immigrants to King County, 2010–2017 [third in nation]
$15.92B	Starbucks 2019 global beverage revenue
15,000	Fishing industry jobs, Washington state
2:1	Sounders titles [MLS] : Seahawks titles [NFL]
$46.8B	Gates Foundation total assets
19	Top Pot Doughnuts locations

NEIGHBORHOODS

BALLARD

Annexed in 1907, this Nordic fishing village retains nautical trappings. Also, Exhibit A of radical neighborhood change.

LOCAL: *Hattie's Hat, Sawyer, Hotel Albatross*

....

FREMONT & WALLINGFORD

Habitat for annual nude bike ride, all-the-time craft brews.

LOCAL: *Dick's Drive-In, the Whale Wins, Kamonegi*

....

UNIVERSITY DISTRICT

"The Ave," the U of W zone's main drag, lines up creaky bars, dining and thrift shops.

LOCAL: *Bulldog News, College Inn Pub, Korean Tofu House*

....

CAPITOL HILL

Music venues, boutiques, gay bars, restaurants and general Seattle-ness.

LOCAL: *Oddfellows, Comet Tavern, Marjorie, La Dive*

....

DOWNTOWN & BELLTOWN

The high-rise core blends with Belltown's ragtag bars, restaurants and sidewalk revelers.

LOCAL: *Rob Roy, Neon Boots*

PIONEER SQUARE

Seattle's oldest address. Vintage brick houses, art galleries, cocktail lounges.

LOCAL: *The London Plane, Arundel Books*

....

INTERNATIONAL DISTRICT

Including Chinatown, Japantown and Little Saigon, the ID is Seattle's most diverse hub.

LOCAL: *Pho Bac Sup Shop, Tsukushinbo, Wing Luke Museum*

....

CENTRAL DISTRICT

The home of beloved Black-owned businesses, now in gentrification flux.

LOCAL: *Chuck's Hop Shop, Fat's Chicken and Waffles, Cafe Selam*

....

WEST SEATTLE

An eclectic cross section, especially along Alki Ave: Seattle-style beach life.

LOCAL: *Pegasus Book Exchange, Harry's Beach House*

....

GEORGETOWN

Rusty zone turned playground of superb bars and makers.

LOCAL: *Georgetown Trailer Park Mall, 9lb Hammer*

o BALLARD   o GREEN LAKE

                UNIVERSITY DISTRICT o
        WALLINGFORD o
                                    LAURELHURST o
            o FREMONT

o MAGNOLIA   LAKE UNION

        o QUEEN ANNE

                    o CAPITOL HILL

            o BELLTOWN
                            MADRONA o
                CENTRAL DISTRICT o
        DOWNTOWN o
    PIONEER SQUARE o   LESCHI o
INTERNATIONAL DISTRICT o

                            ELLIOTT BAY   LAKE WASHINGTON

                                    o MT. BAKER

                            MERCER ISLAND ▷

o WEST SEATTLE   o INDUSTRIAL DISTRICT

                    BEACON HILL o
                        o GEORGETOWN

MORE THAN 80 PICKS ↦

BESTS

A curated list of city favorites—classic and new—from bars and restaurants to shops and experiences, plus a handful of can't-miss experts

FOOD & DRINK

*For more Fish and Seafood,
see our map on page 60.*

ITALIAN
Il Nido
*2717 61st Ave SW
West Seattle*
Lush pasta in a
waterside cabin.
Negroni, buca-
tini special, olive oil
cake. Book early.
....

SUSHI
Sushi Kashiba
*86 Pine St, Ste 1
Downtown*
New post of Seattle's
most celebrated
sushi chef, Shiro
Kashiba. Splurge on
omakase.
....

BREWERY
Holy Mountain
Brewing
*1421 Elliott Ave W
Interbay*
Avant-garde and
Old World draughts.
Blissed-out temple
meets DIY garage.

SEAFOOD
L'Oursin
*1315 E Jefferson St
Central District*
Arctic char tartare is
a wonder. Elevated
seafood, French
technique, natural
wines.
....

SOUTHERN
JuneBaby
*2122 NE 65th St
Ravenna*
A James Beard-
winning homage to
Edouardo Jordan's
Black Southern
heritage.
....

OYSTERS
The Walrus and the
Carpenter
*4743 Ballard Ave NW
Ballard*
The briny Seattle of
lore lives at seafood
virtuosa Renee
Erickson's flagship.

FINE DINING
Canlis
*2576 Aurora Ave N
Queen Anne*
A sleek, modern-
ist fine-dining
landmark. Brilliant
casual pivot during
2020 shutdowns.
....

MEXICAN
La Carta de Oaxaca
*5431 Ballard Ave NW
Ballard*
Oaxacan tacos and
tamales, with a top
chile relleno. Mole
negro is the true
star, though.
....

SERIOUS DIVE
Blue Moon Tavern
*712 NE 45th St
University District*
Ginsberg and Kesey
haunt. Tom Robbins
reportedly crank-
called Picasso from
the pay phone.

CLASSIC CHINESE

Jade Garden
424 7th Ave S
International District
Clamorous dim sum
shrine. Expect a wait
[worth it].

TIKI

Navy Strength
1505 2nd Ave, Ste 102
Belltown
Rummy cocktails,
deconstructed tropical vibe, bánh mì.

CARIBBEAN

Jerk Shack
2510 1st Ave
Downtown
Cutting board half-
chickens, hibiscus-
ginger punch.

FILIPINO

Musang
2524 Beacon Ave S
Beacon Hill
Adobong ribs are the
lutong bahay ["home
cooked"] menu's
don't-miss hit.

FUSION

Stateside
300 E Pike St
Capitol Hill
French-Vietnamese.
Don't skip the chile-
doused pork ribs.

OLD HAUNT

Virginia Inn
1937 1st Ave
Downtown
Go-to bistro and bar
hang since 1903.

SECOND DINNER

Damn the Weather
116 1st Ave S
Pioneer Square
Moody night den
owned by a former
Fleet Fox.

PINTS

Brouwer's Café
400 N 35th St
Fremont
Belgian-style hall, 64
craft beers on tap.

CLASSIC COCKTAILS

Zig Zag Cafe
1501 Western Ave,
Ste 202
Pike Place Market
Helped start the
cocktail revolution,
and still the best
Old-Fashioned.

MEDITERRANEAN

Homer
3013 Beacon Ave S
Beacon Hill
Toothsome
spreads—hummus,
labneh, squash—in a
bright dining room.

BAKERY

Sea Wolf
3621 Stone Way N
Fremont
Rustic breads,
cheese-stuffed lye
rolls, classic ciabatta.

MUSIC AND DRINKS

Life on Mars
722 E Pike St
Capitol Hill
A cocktail named for
a Sigur Rós album
and a "menu" of
vinyl for sale.

VEGETARIAN

Cafe Flora
2901 E Madison St
Madison Valley
Ideal veggie
scrambles even lure
carnivores.

BARBECUE

Emma's
5303 Rainier Ave S
Hillman City
Classic joint with
tangy, tender ribs.

FRIED CHICKEN

Ezell's Famous
Chicken
501 23rd Ave
Central District
Tender legs and
breasts since 1984.
Prized by Oprah.

SHOPPING

GAGS
Archie McPhee
1300 N 45th St
Wallingford
Rubber chickens and whimsical historical action figures are the specialities at this novelty and whatzit stronghold.
....

UMBRELLAS
Certain Standard
3801 Stone Way N, Ste E, Wallingford
Racy, Euro-palette colors and smart design details elevate the bumbershoot.
....

BEAUTY
K Banana
1621 NE Village Ln University District
Importing the latest in sharply packaged Korean beauty gear. A sunbeam of cuteness on gray days.

OLD VINYL
Daybreak Records
4323 Fremont Ave N Fremont
Exacting curation and well-appointed listening for rarities in all genres, and a fun social-media follow for vinyl lovers.
....

SLEEPING BAGS
Feathered Friends
263 Yale Ave N Downtown
Pods of warmth and aesthetic excellence, prized in the high country since 1972.
....

JAPANESE DENIM
Blue Owl Workshop
124 NW Canal St, Ste 1, Fremont
Stacks of imported selvedge and Japanese brands, plus the insanely detailed "Fade Museum."

NEW VINYL
Easy Street Records
4559 California Ave SW, West Seattle
Streaming be damned, this neighborhood staple has a citywide cred for its all-genres horde of new and used.
....

UNISEX STYLES
Glasswing
1525 Melrose Ave Capitol Hill
Across all genders, flowy, organic looks with workwear roots. [Lush plants, too.]

ASIAN SUPERMARKET
Uwajimaya
600 5th Ave S International District
A completist's trove of Asian pantry, saké galore, Sanrio swag, import magazines and superb seafood.

OUTERWEAR

Outdoor Research
2203 1st Ave S
South Seattle
A rangy line of rugged, Seattle-made cold-weather repellers.

....

FURNITURE

Sparklebarn
1611 NW Market St
Ballard
Midcentury-ish vintage, high in quality but playful.

....

JEWELRY

Valerie Madison
1411 34th Ave
Madrona
All-local production, luxe meets boho.

....

PANTRY

Big John's PFI
1608 S Dearborn St
South Seattle
A serious cook's back-street source for cheese, pasta, salami and wine.

....

WINE SHOP

Bottlehouse
1416 34th Ave
Madrona
A shop and bar emphasizes local and natural bottles.

ARTS MATERIALS

Daniel Smith
4150 1st Ave S
South Seattle
A noted and innovative maker of watercolors and oils.

....

SURVIVAL SUPPLIER

Federal Army & Navy Surplus
2112 1st Ave
Belltown
MREs, pirate flags, random ruggedness.

....

DEPARTMENT STORE

Nordstrom
500 Pine St
Downtown
Founded by a Swedish immigrant, funded by Yukon gold.

....

WOMENSWEAR

Lika Love
535 Warren Ave N
Queen Anne Hill
Zesty haute-casual looks, from storefront or truck.

....

PLANTS

City People's Garden Store
2939 E Madison St
Madison Valley
Shrubs, herbs and succulents fit for the apocalypse.

VINTAGE

Kirk Albert
5517 Airport Way S
Georgetown
Gallery-quality art, furniture and objets.

....

MENSWEAR

Division Road
536 1st Ave S
Pioneer Square
A handsome stock of heritage-oriented brands and collaborations to evoke the rustic and retro.

....

SWISS ARMY KNIFE

Wayward
204 Pine St
Downtown
Cameras to T-shirts to duffels: cool gear dreams fulfilled.

....

INSTRUMENTS

Dusty Strings
3406 Fremont Ave N
Fremont
Axes in all flavors, plus ukes and house-made dulcimers.

....

VIDEO

Scarecrow
5030 Roosevelt Way NE
University District
"The world's largest video library": 117,000-plus titles.

ACTION

SOCCER
OL Reign
Cheney Stadium, Tacoma
Local pros, affiliated with French titan Olympique Lyonnais. Megan Rapinoe runs the wing.
....

CULTURAL CENTER
Langston
104 17th Ave S Central District
A focal point for Black performance and other arts, home to the Seattle Black Film Festival.
....

SEA CHANTEYS
NW Seaport Maritime Heritage Center
860 Terry Ave N Lake Union
Gather to sing sailorly odes at a historic fleet's home.

FUTURIST TRANSPORT
Seattle Center Monorail
Westlake Center Mall Downtown
Jetsons-esque local icon, built for the '62 world's fair. Short trip but worth the ride.
....

URBAN BEACH
Golden Gardens Park
8498 Seaview Pl NW Ballard
A sweeping, popular park and gateway to a utopian coast, with Sound, island and Olympic views.
....

CHORAL SINGING
Saint Mark's Episcopal Cathedral
1245 10th Ave E Capitol Hill
Sunday compline service brings hundreds to this progressive faith center.

CINEMA
SIFF Cinema Uptown
511 Queen Anne Ave N, Downtown
Art house anchor of Seattle International Film Festival's programs.
....

PUBLIC POOL
Colman
8603 Fauntleroy Way SW, West Seattle
A saltwater stunner. Outdoors, Olympic-size and set by a Sound beach. Giant tube slide.
....

LIVE GIGS
Neumos
123 Address Capitol Hill
An intimate space hosts the best indie and hip-hop shows. Pronounced "new moe's."

EXPEDITION
Hoh Rain Forest
Olympic National Park
Trek four hours to America's quietest [and mossiest?] spot.
....

KARAOKE
Rock Box
1603 Nagle Pl Capitol Hill
Twelve Japanese-style private chambers.
....

VINTAGE MOTORCYCLES
MotoShed
3208 Queen Anne Ave N, Queen Anne
Pro repairs, DIY memberships, coffee shop the Wick.
....

DAY HIKE
Oyster Dome
Chuckanut Area wta.org
Mountains meet Sound, 90 minutes north.
....

CONTEMPORARY ART
Foster/White
220 3rd Ave S Pioneer Square
Hyper-local painting and photography, perception-bending sculpture.

GAY BAR
Pony
1221 E Madison St Capitol Hill
A tiny stronghold of unabashed grit. "A very gay bar."
....

SEAHAWKS BAR
Quality Athletics
121 S King St Pioneer Square
Elevated pub grub. Screens galore.
....

X-COUNTRY SKIING
The Summit at Snoqualmie
Snoqualmie Pass summitatsnoqualmie.com
Fifty groomed kilometers, an hour from town.
....

SOUNDERS BAR
The Dray
708 NW 65th St Phinney Ridge
Woodsy snug with Eurobeers on tap.
....

ODDITIES
Fremont Troll and Lenin statues
Fremont
A self-guided stroll from the Bridge beast to the Bolshevik capo keeps plinths weird.

WEEKLY RUN
Super Jock 'n Jill
7210 E Green Lake Dr N, Green Lake
Social evening outings circle an urban lake, about 3 miles.
....

ARCADE
Seattle Pinball Museum
508 Maynard Ave S International District
Bargain all-day play on vintage machines.
....

OPEN-WATER SWIM
Park to Park
Lake Washington parktoparkswim.com
August plunge, one way or out and back.
....

MINOR LEAGUE BALL
Everett AquaSox
Funko Field, Everett
Class A action in a chill suburban ballpark. Watch for Webbly.
....

MOUNTAIN RETREAT
Lake Crescent Lodge
Olympic National Park
Rustic 1915 classic with cozy fire, shoreline cabins.

EXPERTISE

BRANDING

Terry Heckler
hecklerbranding.com
His agency unleashed the "Wild Rainiers" of '70s beer ads [now YouTube candy]. He sketched the Starbucks mermaid.

....

INDIGENOUS ART

Yəhaw
yehawshow.com
An experimental and public-art collective curates Native shows and programs with activist aims.

....

SCANDI-HISTORY

National Nordic Museum
nordicmuseum.org
An airy examination of culture, history and politics in Ballard. Publishes *Nordic Kultur*.

SEA MAMMALS

Kenneth Balcomb
whaleresearch.com
From an island base in Friday Harbor, his organization leads research on the critically endangered Southern Resident orca pod.

....

CEPHALOPODS

Kathryn Kegel
seattleaquarium.org
The octopi authority in a town where that means something, she directs divers in an annual census.

....

WRITING CLASSES

Hugo House
1634 11th Ave
hugohouse.org
Curriculum for prose and verse. Named for noted Northwest poet Richard Hugo.

SKATEBOARDS

Subsonic
subsonicskateboards.com
Custom and production longboards, with an emphasis on designs for long-distance rides and ballistic downhill speed.

....

NATURAL HISTORY

Burke Museum
seattleaquarium.org
A newly rebuilt center for flora, fauna and human culture reinvents the natural history museum.

....

SIGNAGE

Western Neon
westernneon.com
Innovative and precise tube-benders of choice, with work aglow everywhere. See the color-shifting City Light sign.

SOCIAL CHANGE

Ijeoma Oluo

Ijeomaoluo.com

Her book *So You Want to Talk About Race* became a national must-read during 2020's reckoning.

....

CARTOGRAPHY

Metsker Maps

metskers.com

Which map do you need? Navigational source since 1950.

....

KNIFE SHARPENING

Seattle Edge

knifesharpening seattle.com

Rare blades, classes and hand-honing, $2 per inch.

....

ART & CULTURE

Northwest African American Museum

naamnw.org

The Central District home of contemporary art and regional Black history.

....

GIFT CONCIERGE

Alair

alairseattle.com

Bespoke packages, tailored to suit someone lucky.

HISTORY

Ghosts of Seattle Past

seattleghosts.com

Acclaimed atlas of lost cityscapes.

....

TATTOOS

Tattoos and Fortune

tattoosandfortune.com

Woman-owned, Capitol Hill-based black-ink specialist.

....

WINEMAKER

Charles Smith

charlessmithwines.com

A former rock band manager bottles all-WA grapes. Kung Fu Girl Riesling and Velvet Devil Merlot both score high.

....

ASIAN ART

SAAM

seattleartmuseum.org

The newly renovated Volunteer Park trove curates outside geographic and chronological boundaries.

....

NAUTICAL CHARTS

Captain's Supplies

captainsnautical.com

Seafarers' guides from the Admiralty, NOAA and more.

GAME DESIGN

Wizards of the Coast

wizards.com

Makers of *Magic: The Gathering* and *Dungeons & Dragons*.

....

OP-ED

Timothy Egan

timothyeganbooks.com

His *NYT* columns put Seattle's lens on national affairs.

....

CONTRACTOR

Dovetail

dovetailgc.com

Call them to execute that modernist forest cabin you ponder.

....

GRAPHIC NOVELS

Ellen Forney

ellenforney.com

Inked stories with mental-health focus.

....

LANGUAGE

Tulalip Lushootseed Department

tulaliplushootseed.com

Portal for a tribal alphabet, phrases.

....

LANDSCAPING

Ohashi

ohashilandscape.com

Lush, mod, Asian-influenced grounds.

MORE THAN 30 ENTRIES ▷

ALMANAC

---

*A deep dive into the cultural heritage of
Seattle through news clippings, lost letters, timelines,
journal entries and other historical hearsay*

SEATTLE MILESTONES

1851 ..... Early settlement New York Alki [Chinook for "someday"]

1855 ..... Treaty of Point Elliott: U.S. takes Native lands

1860s... Yesler Way nicknamed "Skid Road"

1886 .... First African Methodist Episcopal Church founded

1896.....*Miike Maru*, first Japan-North America ocean liner

1897..... Klondike Gold Rush turns Seattle into Alaska logistics hub

1907 .... American Messenger Company founded. Becomes UPS.

1916 ..... Boatbuilder Bill Boeing co-founds Pacific Aero Products Co.

1919 ..... Flu pandemic ends Seattle Metropolitans' run at Stanley Cup

1926 ..... Bertha Knight Landes: America's first female big-city mayor

1941 ..... War sparks migration: Black population quadruples by 1950

1942 ..... Japanese American citizens interned by federal order

1962 ..... The Century 21 Exposition brings Space Needle, Monorail

..... Wing Luke: first Chinese American city council member

1967......*Seattle* cover: Peter Wichern, businessman, "homosexual"

1969 .... Seattle Pilots' sole Major League year feeds Bouton's *Ball Four*

1976 ..... Seattle Seahawks finish first year 2-12

1979 ..... Seattle SuperSonics win only NBA title

..... Microsoft relocates from Albuquerque to suburban Redmond

1989 ..... "Paddle to Seattle" reinvigorates Native canoe voyaging

1991 ..... Sex advice column "Savage Love" debuts in *The Stranger*

1992 ..... Marc Jacobs sends noted "grunge collection" to catwalk

1993 .....*Frasier* debuts on NBC

.....*Bill Nye the Science Guy* debuts on KCTS

2003..... Starbucks introduces the Pumpkin Spice Latte

2005 .... Amazon Prime launches as expedited shipping offer

....*Grey's Anatomy* debuts on ABC

2008 .... SuperSonics relocate to Oklahoma City

2013 ..... Lushootseed language revival efforts in full swing

2014 .... Wilson/Lynch/Sherman Seahawks win Super Bowl

2018..... Pramila Jayapal: first Indian American woman in Congress

2020 .... UW releases oft-cited coronavirus data

.... "Free Capitol Hill" declared during Black Lives Matter protests

GOLD RUSH

The Seattle Post-Intelligencer, July 17, 1897

"LATEST NEWS FROM THE KLONDIKE."

GOLD! GOLD! GOLD! GOLD!
Sixty-Eight Rich Men on the Steamer Portland.

STACKS OF YELLOW METAL!
Some Have $5,000, Many Have More, and a
Few Bring Out $100,000 Each.

At 3 o'clock this morning the steamship Portland, from St. Michaels for Seattle, passed up the Sound with more than a ton of solid gold on board and 68 passengers. In the captain's cabin are three chests and a large safe filled with the precious nuggets. ... In size the nuggets range from the size of a pea to a guinea egg. ... One peculiar feature to be noticed is that the big strikes were made by tenderfeet, while the old and experienced miners of many years' experience are suffering indescribable hardship and privation in Alaska and the Northwest Territory and have only a few thousand dollars to show for their labor. Fortune seemed to smile on the inexperienced men who went into the mining districts late last year, as nearly all of them were the most fortunate. The stories they tell seem too incredulous and far beyond belief. Instances are noted where single individuals have taken out, in two and one-half months, gold to the value of over $150,000. ... [T]hey all advise and urge people who contemplate going to the Yukon not to think of taking in less than one ton of grub, and plenty of clothes.

MUSICIANS OF NOTE

Kurt Cobain	Logging town kid's angry yowl, guitar gnarls defined Seattle's signature rock sound of the early '90s.
Ray Charles	Formative '40s gigs at the Rocking Chair, "Confession Blues" recording session.
Quincy Jones	Ray's protégé. Newspaper quote: "Seattle in the 1940s was like New Orleans."
Ernestine Anderson	Broke big in the hot Jackson Street jazz scene while still a teenager.
Geoff Tate	Before grunge, hair metal. Queensrÿche frontman banged heads with the best.
Ann and Nancy Wilson	Sisters at the heart of Heart. "Magic Man," "Crazy on You" both charted in '76.
Mia Zapata	The Gits frontwoman wielded epic punk presence. Tragically murdered in 1993.
Brandi Carlile	Sweet-voiced country star from tiny Ravensdale. Highwomen co-founder, LGBTQ icon.
Dave Matthews	The South Africa-born jam-popster is a low-key [seldom embraced] transplant.
Jimi Hendrix	Born and schooled here, meteoric career elsewhere. Buried at Greenwood cemetery, Renton.
Macklemore	It took a Seattle MC to write hip-hop's paean to thrift-store shopping and 99-cent finds.
Robin Pecknold	Fleet Foxes leader, from suburban Kirkland, sometimes aka White Antelope.
Neko Case	Early career breakthrough here. "South Tacoma Way" remains an I-5 corridor ode.
Ishmael Butler	Jazz/hip-hop fusionist with Digable Planets, now Shabazz Palaces mainstay. Father of Lil Tracy.
TAD	Tad Doyle, hirsute and hulking, embodies the gruffest side of grunge.

RAIN

TOM ROBBINS
Still Life With Woodpecker

"On the mainland, a rain was falling. The famous Seattle rain. The thin, gray rain that toadstools love. The persistent rain that knows every hidden entrance into collar and shopping bag. The quiet rain that can rust a tin roof without the tin roof making a sound in protest. The shamanic rain that feeds the imagination. The rain that seems actually a secret language, whispering, like the ecstasy of primitives, of the essence of things."

···

WILLIAM CLARK
Lewis and Clark Expedition journal, December 16, 1805

"The rain Continues, with Tremendous gusts of wind ... The winds violent. Trees falling in every direction, whorl winds, with gusts of rain Hail & Thunder, this kind of weather lasted all day, Certainly one of the worst days that ever was!"

···

MARIA SEMPLE
Where'd You Go, Bernadette

"Let's play a game. I'll say a word, and you say the first word that pops into your head. Ready? ME: Seattle. YOU: Rain. What you've heard about the rain: it's all true. So you'd think it would become part of the fabric, especially among the lifers. But every time it rains, and you have to interact with someone, here's what they'll say: 'Can you believe the weather?' And you want to say, 'Actually, I can believe the weather. What I can't believe is that I'm actually having a conversation about the weather.' But I don't say that, you see, because that would be instigating a fight, something I try my best to avoid, with mixed results."

···

TIMOTHY EGAN
The Good Rain

"The rain has always been the secret weapon. Winter days can be so dark and dank that a flashlight is helpful on a midday stroll. For nine months out of the year meteorologists issue one basic forecast: rain turning to showers. Turning to showers? How can they tell? The clouds are seldom forceful and usually tentative. The volume is nothing unusual—less rain falls here than in any city on the East Coast—it's the threat, the constant ambiguity in the sky, that drives people crazy."

ANTI-CHINESE RIOT

Harper's Weekly
March 6, 1886

A deliberate and determined effort … was made on Sunday, February 7, to expel the Chinese from the town of Seattle, Washington Territory. By a preconcerted plan, of which neither the law-abiding citizens of the town nor the Chinamen had a hint, a mob invaded the Chinese quarter late Saturday night, forcibly but quietly entered the houses, dragged the occupants from their beds, forced them quickly to pack their personal effects, and marched them to a steamer. … The few policemen that became aware of the wrong-doing had no power and slight willingness to prevent it, and before the sleeping citizens of the town or the county officers knew what was going on, 400 Chinamen were shivering on the dock.

BOEING PLANES

B & W	Wooden seaplane built on Lake Union, 1916
MODEL C	Co-designed by Beijing-born engineer Wong Tsu for WWI
B-17	The Flying Fortress: Dominated WWII aerial theater
707	First jetliner, in service for Pan Am by 1958
717	Slim 100-seater, 1999–2006
727	A compromise of three airlines' specs; retired in 1984
737	A mid-'60s short-haul design; 15,000 delivered as of 2019
747	Designed to meet Jet Age demand, doubles 707's capacity
757	Post-oil crisis 727 replacement and domestic workhorse
767	1980s-born long-hauler; transatlantic staple
777	Modern long-distance model with international appeal
787	The "Dreamliner" of fuel efficiency aspirations
737 MAX	Two tragic crashes left this latter-day update grounded in 2019

> *At a 1966 ceremony celebrating the 747, Pan Am founder Juan Trippe foretold that the plane would be "a great weapon for peace, competing with intercontinental ballistic missiles for mankind's destiny."*

BATTLE OF SEATTLE

Harry A. Smith, January 1856

The Indians had no doubt been watching our movements for the very next morning, the 26th, they made an attack upon the town and the *Decatur* a U.S. man o' war [attack was made at 8 o'clock a.m.]. Marines from here were landed and fired into the woods across the tide marsh ... that separated Seattle from the hill to the east. War whoops filled the woods with thunder—so securely did the Indians keep themselves hid from sight that only glimpses of them as they dodged from one tree to another could be seen. They numbered eight or ten hundred as was afterwards learned. The woods resounded all day and their thunderous yells in a continuous roar from Mr. Bell's house to Hanford's, a distance of two miles. Their plan was to make the attack while our citizens were at breakfast and ... surprise and murder them before they could rally for defense. Friendly Indians betrayed the plot and the captain of the *Decatur* determined to test the truth of the report by firing a few random howitzer shots into the dense woods. The firing caused the Indians to think they were discovered and they soon returned the fire with Hudson Bay muskets with which they were well armed. ...

The ship's howitzer blazed away all day. The marines and volunteers first mustered out of service kept up a firing all day while the *Decatur* fired broad side after broad side of shot and shell tearing limbs and bark from the trees and shore. Yet so determined were the Indians that they kept up their firing until darkness hid the town from view. All was silence save for the hootings like owls, the signals from one chief to another. They ... gave up all hopes of capturing the town and contented themselves with drawing off all the stock and burning nearly every house in the surrounding country. On the 28 of Jan., a new company was formed called Co. A, Captain Landin and First Lieutenant A.A. Denny. He returned to the fort on the bank of the Duwamish river and made it headquarters for six months, then [the] company was discharged.

This conflict ultimately led to the arrest of Leschi, a Nisqually chief, and his brother, Quiemuth. Quiemuth was mysteriously murdered in the territorial governor's office. Leschi was convicted of murder and hanged after a trial marked by irregularities. The state exonerated him in 2004.

TED BUNDY

The Seattle Times
October 3, 1975

"Ted Bundy—very bright ... ethical ... super nice guy ... an all-American boy." That was the picture that emerged here yesterday after the news broke that Bundy was charged in Salt Lake City with kidnapping and attempted murder in connection with the abduction of a teen-age girl in Utah last November. Those who knew Theodore R. Bundy, a University of Utah law student who was a special aide to the re-election campaign of Gov. Dan Evans in 1972, said the news was hard to believe. Bundy, 28, a former Tacoman who had lived in Seattle, in 1972 also was assistant director of the Seattle Crime Prevention Advisory Commission ... "It just doesn't make any sense," said Ross Davis, chairman of the Republican State Central Committee. "I have a terrible time, personally, believing it ... It's not the Ted Bundy I know. Either something happened to him in the meantime or somebody's made a terrible mistake." ... Mrs. Patti Adams, who manages an apartment house near where Bundy lived in the University District, said: "Ted was like a son to Mr. and Mrs. Roger. After Mr. Roger became ill, Ted mowed and took care of their yard and helped take care of Mr. Roger." Mrs. Adams described Bundy as "a very good looking young man who was super nice to all of us." She said she knew him on a neighborly basis for about four years. Mrs. Roger said that Bundy drove a Volkswagen Beetle that was "tan in color." In investigating a 1974 series of women who are missing or murdered in Washington, police have sought a young man who identified himself as "Ted" when he approached several women at Lake Sammamish State Park in July 1974. He was described as having a brown Volkswagen.

Linked to dozens of horrific crimes, Bundy became a cultural byword in the 1980s and a case study in pathology. Among the large collection of Bundy-related films, books and television shows, Ann Rule's 1980 book The Stranger Beside Me *remains arguably best-known.*

WORLD TRADE ORGANIZATION PROTESTS

In 1999, huge protests greeted the WTO Ministerial Conference in Seattle, reverberating globally and informing decades of activism.

JANUARY 25 Seattle selected as WTO host. Wealthy and developing nations divided on "Millennium Round" of global trade-rules talks.

....

JULY 16 *Wall Street Journal*: "Globalization Foes Plan to Protest WTO's Seattle Round Trade Talks."

....

SEPTEMPBER 13 Mayor Paul Schell requests federal security for the November conference: "threat situation" is "fluid and temperamental."

....

NOVEMBER 24 Thousands of *Seattle Post-Intelligencer* spoof copies appear on streets, delivering brutal anti-WTO satire and hinting at protest scale.

....

NOVEMBER 29 Peaceful protests, with sea turtle costumes worn. Sign: "DEFEND OUR FORESTS, CLEARCUT THE WTO."

....

NOVEMBER 30 "N30": Activists seize key downtown intersections. Police fire tear gas, munitions. Anarchists blamed for violence, property damage.

....

DECEMBER 1 Capitol Hill confrontations: "Off our hill!" chants. President Clinton arrives. National Guard deploys. Steelworkers march.

....

DECEMBER 2 Tensions ease as Clinton departs and police use less force. Protests continue at King County Jail, elsewhere.

....

DECEMBER 3 WTO talks collapse without agreement on key issues. [Ministers convene in protest-free Qatar in 2001, launch "Doha Round."]

THE INFERNAL NOISE BRIGADE, *a street protest percussion band, debuted for WTO. Christopher Frizzelle of* The Stranger *reported from the group's 2006 "funeral": "[M]ourners sat on top of an old school bus, but most stood on the uneven terrain ... getting their suits and dresses dirty, drinking whiskey or beer or homemade mead, rolling cigarettes, smoking joints, chewing chocolates packed with mushrooms."*

CROWS

If Seattle has a true mascot, it's the crow. The birds are ubiquitous—silhouettes always in the periphery, on power lines, atop fences, swooping across parking lots and divebombing pedestrians, black-clad aviators with attitude. The city's geography, essentially urban pockets grafted onto lush forests and hemmed in by two bodies of water, provides perfect habitat for *Corvus brachyrhynchos*, especially in Capitol Hill, where the feathered beasts stalk the sidewalks like hungover revelers the morning after. Seattle's also home to the most significant corvid research of the past two decades. University of Washington scientists have demonstrated [in an experiment employing Dick Cheney masks] that crows recognize and remember individual human faces. The birds use found objects as tools and mourn their dead. Animal behaviorist Dr. Kaeli Swift has shown that they hold funerals by taking flight, en masse, above the corpse and circling it in a terrifying, surround-sound chorus of shrieks and caws, and that particularly amorous specimens will attempt copulation with the fallen bird.

BUTTERWORTH & SONS

Edgar Ray Butterworth [1847-1921] turned mourning into big business, revolutionizing the funerary trade. [He's credited with popularizing "mortician," a marketing term supplanting "undertaker."] In 1903, the family firm opened new digs.

Butterworth & Sons, the undertakers, have moved into their new building, 1921 First Avenue, two blocks above Pike Street. In their new quarters they claim to have the most complete establishment in the United States. They occupy five floors with a building area of 30 x 112 feet. The first floor or basement is used for horses and vehicles and necessary appurtenances belonging thereto. The second floor consists of a stock room and five receiving vaults. ... The chapel is finished in Flemish oak, with seating pews of same finish. Two features of the chapel are new and unique, one of them being a choir loft and balcony which seats fifty people. The chapel will accommodate comfortably 200 persons. In the rear of the chapel is the mourners' or family room, which is reached by private entrance. The display of caskets is segregated in four different rooms. The establishment has a private and public morgue. The building is admirably adapted for its purpose and complete in all its details. —*The Seattle Sunday Times,* October 11, 1903

PIKE PLACE MARKET

Seattle established Pike Place Market, the iconic city-center farmers market, in 1907. Since then, the Market has been both a symbol of urban vitality and a perennial political issue.

LETTER TO CITY COUNCIL, JANUARY 20, 1921

The management of the Farmers' Public Market is a difficult problem. They violate the rules and we are called upon frequently to suspend different farmers for such violation. … It will be necessary to have at least two men with proper transportation facilities to ferret out those who do crooked work and check up on farmers who appear on the market. It will take these men all their time to visit the farms twice or three times a year … I, therefore, request you to amend the existing ordinance to allow us to charge 25¢ per day for each stall and to draft and pass an ordinance that will permit the employment of two additional market inspectors properly equipped with transportation.
—*H.M. Read, Commissioner of Health*

....

In 1971, commercial real estate investors proposed redeveloping the Market. [Plans looked akin to a mixed-use shopping mall.] Preservationists, led by Space Needle architect Victor Steinbrueck and cheered on by eminent newspaper columnist Emmett Watson, passed Initiative No. 1, establishing a 7-acre historic district.

Seattle Post-Intelligencer
November 1, 1971

The Market, to me, is a living thing. It is a babble of voices, different languages, different accents. It is the incredibly beautiful displays and colors of vegetables; its very tackiness is part of its charm and a living reassurance that things are not all plastic in this Saran-wrapped world. The Market is the smell of beer and fresh bread and fish; it is the noise of the feet shuffling along the stall, the cry of the hucksters, the popping of bags, the laughter in the air, the bar of music that makes a city … People know about Seattle because of the Market, and I am desperately afraid that any giant project of parking lots, hotels and apartments will destroy this fragile thing that has made Seattle famous. —*Emmett Watson*

PETER PUGET'S JOURNAL

From A Log of the proceedings of His Majesty's Sloop *Discovery*, George
Vancouver Esqre, Commander, *May* 9, 1792

—At Day Light we looked around with Anxiety to ascertain what kind of
a Situation we had fixt on, as on the preceding Evening the Fire Arms had
got wet & even not yet put in Order that should this Station have been near
a large Village we would have proved but a Weak force—But we appeared to
have pitched in a very eligible Spot, it was a Snug cove … During the whole
of the 9th it Rained & blew hard which prevented our moving, we therefore
employed in putting the Fire Arms in order—The Surrounding Country
appears like a thick Forest of Pines it is low— abounds near the Beaches
with some very pleasant Spots—In this Cove were some Small Oak Trees,
Maple, Pines of various Sorts, Gooseberry & Raspberry Bushes—Of Birds,
there were the White Headed & Brown Eagle, Crows Ravens Curlews &
some Oceanic Birds—At Low Water the Beaches afforded us an Excellent
Supply of Clams but a Small Seine we had was unsuccessful—

> *Vancouver's crew—Lieutenant Puget was a trusted officer—crossed
> paths with Spanish and American ships, all seeking the fabled Northwest
> Passage and imperial advantage. The British expedition established the
> European names of numerous natural features and places.*

SIR MIX-A-LOT'S "POSSE ON BROADWAY"

In 1988*, the rapper Sir Mix-A-Lot turned a ordinary night out into an epic
tale. Arguably Seattle's first hip-hop hit, its itinerary is local legend.*

RAINIER AVE Mix-A-Lot "rolling" in a black Mercedes-Benz with cellular phone.

23RD AND JACKSON Posse gathers, seeks action, heads for strip [Broadway].

MLK WAY "Set looks kinda dead."

23RD AVE Mix-A-Lot assesses crack scourge. Driver breaks left.

BROADWAY "Time to get ill."

"COLLEGE" Seattle Central College: Women crowd available car space.

TACO BELL Posse finds location [now defunct] closed.

DICK'S Fast-food go-to draws crowd. Hater maced. His companion joins posse.

BEAT IMPRESSIONS

JACK KEROUAC
From *Lonesome Traveler* [1960]

"Anybody who's been to Seattle and missed Alaskan Way, the old water front, has missed the point—here the totem-pole stores, the waters of Puget Sound washing under old piers, the dark gloomy look of ancient warehouses and pier sheds, and the most antique locomotives in America switching boxcars up and down the water front, give a hint, under the pure cloud-mopped sparkling skies of the Northwest, of great country to come."

ALLEN GINSBERG
From "Afternoon Seattle" [1956]

"Labyrinth wood stairways and Greek movies under Farmers Market second hand city, Indian smoked salmon old overcoats and dry red shoes, / Green Parrot Theater, Maytime, and down to the harborside the ships, walked on Alaska silent together—ferry-boat coming faraway in mist from Bremerton Island dreamlike small ... / —and entered my head the seagull, a shriek, sentinels standing over rusty harbor iron dock-work, rocks dripping under rotten wharves slime on the walls—"

PELLEGRINI

UW professor and peer of Beard and Child, Angelo Pellegrini advocated a new American food culture. [He authored the nation's first pesto recipe in Sunset *magazine in 1946]. From his 1948 manifesto,* The Unprejudiced Palate:

Only the most complacent provincial would deny that American cuisine can be vastly improved; that—and this needs emphasis—the American's whole attitude toward food and drink leaves much to be desired ... Those, however, who look to Europe for instruction in cooking must studiously avoid the fakirs, the gastronomic sensationalists, the apostles of culinary decadence. Too often, the cuisine these immature gourmets write about is precious and extravagant. It is the cuisine of the idle rich, foreign and domestic, designed to give new thrills and new excitements to pitiful souls who have never known the enduring joy of an honest, productive life. It is the cuisine of consecutive courses, accompanied by a variety of wines, white and red, still and sparkling, followed by exotic desserts and an array of liqueurs.

THE SEAHAWKS

"Seismologists say Seahawks fans shook the ground under Seattle's CenturyLink Field during Saturday's defeat of the New Orleans Saints ... The scientists believe the small earthquake during a Marshawn Lynch touchdown was likely greater than Lynch's famous 'beast quake' touchdown run three years ago, which also came against New Orleans during a playoff game. ... Fans jumped and stomped their way to a magnitude 1 or 2 earthquake in 2011 during Lynch's rambling, tackle-breaking 'beast quake' run."
—*Associated Press, January 12, 2014*

FORT LAWTON OCCUPATION

In spring 1970, United Indians of All Tribes attempted to occupy Fort Lawton, an Army base in Seattle's Magnolia neighborhood. In April, the Indian Center News *reported:*

United Indians of All Tribes, after a three-week assault on the army post at Fort Lawton, have folded their teepees and retired to warmer quarters to continue their effort to win support for their claim to the land which the army will shortly evacuate. The non-violent invasion, which included three efforts to set up an encampment within the fort, accomplished the UIAT goal of bringing the plight of urban Indians to the attention of officials and the public. Each invasion was marked by the reading of the UIAT proclamation ... We, the native Americans, re-claim the land known as Fort Lawton in the name of all American Indians by the right of discovery.

> *The UIAT proposed creating a cultural and educational center. Ultimately, Fort Lawton became Discovery Park and included the Daybreak Star Indian Cultural Center, UIAT's present headquarters.*

BILLIONAIRES

JEFF BEZOS

"There's a big, new bookstore in town, and there's a catch—you won't find it on any Seattle street map. So if you want to wander down its aisles and peruse the selection, you'll have to hook up to the Internet. That's what Jeff Bezos, 31, the founder of Amazon.com Books is gambling on—that book lovers the world over will drop in, check out his new Web site and get hooked. He's able to provide customers with a searchable database of more than 1 million titles. ... Since Amazon—named after the longest river in the Western Hemisphere—doesn't require selling space, it is able to offer customers a selection of books that is larger than what most bookstores offer, Bezos said. Its motto is 'If it's in print, it's in stock.'" —*The Seattle Times, September 19, 1995*

BILL GATES

"First inquisitively, then eagerly, then passionately, the two schoolboys typed commands to a computer in Seattle 14 years ago. They were enthralled by the power too and struck by their control over it. In the first week, they used $3,000 worth of computer time—the school's entire allotment for the year. Officials at the private Lakeside School were less than pleased to see their computer budget blown. But Bill Gates, who was in seventh grade, and Paul Allen, who was in ninth, were undaunted. They taught the computer to play Monopoly, and then commanded it to play millions of games to discover strategies which tended to succeed." —*The Seattle Times, February 14, 1982*

HOWARD SCHULTZ

"What happens when a popular, well-established coffee company is bought by a sexy, upstart chain of Italian espresso shops? You get a company that could one day make people in Chicago and Boston as picky about their lattes, cappuccinos and Viennese blend beans as coffee drinkers in Seattle. At least that's Howard Schultz's plan. Schultz, president and a principal owner of Il Giornale Coffee Co., a chain of four Seattle and Vancouver B.C. espresso shops, three weeks ago bought Starbucks Coffee Co., the Seattle company whose name is synonymous with gourmet coffee. Starbucks was started in 1971. Schultz wants to open Starbucks stores and Il Giornale espresso bars nationwide with hopes that the same people who drop by an Il Giornale on their way to work will stop off to pick up gourmet coffee at a Starbucks store on their way home. 'Our main goal is to position Starbucks coffee as the first national brand of specialty coffee,' Schultz said." —*The Seattle Times, June 16, 1987*

EDWARD CURTIS

Starting in Seattle in 1887, Curtis created perhaps the most iconic photographs of Native Americans, devoting decades to his series The North American Indian. *In 1949, he wrote out answers to Seattle librarian Harriet Leitch's questions about his early days.*

LEITCH: How many years in Seattle?
CURTIS: About twenty-five … Had a family to support. A spinal injury made it impossible to work in lumber yards. Knowing a little about photography, I bought an interest in a small photo shop.

LEITCH: But how did you start?
CURTIS: Went to the Tulalip Reservation early one a.m., hired the Indian policeman and his wife for the day and made some portraits. Went back another day and made some more.

LEITCH: How did you get the confidence of the Indians?
CURTIS: I said "we," not "you." In other words, I worked with them, not at them.

—For an examination of Curtis' life and artistic legacy, see Timothy Egan's Short Nights of the Shadow Catcher [2012].

THE SEATTLE DOG

In a city hardly known for street fare, the most singular foodway is a hot dog slung from carts long after midnight. Even calling this a "hot dog" is like calling Jimi Hendrix a mere guitarist; like its fellow child of the city, the Seattle Dog sets genres on fire. Its most shocking premise: What if all hot dogs came smeared with cream cheese? To that blasphemy, add a welter of grilled onions and a swollen Polish sausage laid down on a toasty bun. Procured nightly outside concert venues like Neumos and the Crocodile, and on practically every bar-studded Belltown and Capitol Hill block in between, a Seattle Dog is best enjoyed several Rainiers in and eardrums ringing. But that advice hides a fundamental truth about this totem of Seattle nightlife. The cream cheese is cold, the sausage link and onions hot, and that clash of temperatures, along with all those competing textures, makes for an unforgettable bite. You'll remember it long after the house lights blaze on, and the streets fill with wobbly pedestrians and then empty, and to the east the horizon begins to pale.

FAKE GRUNGE LEXICON

In 1992, as Seattle's music scene boomed, The New York Times *called pivotal local label Sub Pop for insight. Megan Jasper—friend of Sub Pop Records' founders and, today, the label's CEO—answered, improvising a bogus slang vocabulary dutifully reprinted by* The Times.

WACK SLACKS ....Old ripped jeans

FUZZ ....Heavy wool sweaters

PLATS ....Platform shoes

KICKERS ....Heavy boots

SWINGIN' ON THE FLIPPITY-FLOP .... Hanging out

BOUND-AND-HAGGED .... Staying home on Friday or Saturday night

SCORE .... Great

HARSH REALM .... Bummer

COB NOBBLER ....Loser

DISH ....Desirable guy

BLOATED, BIG BAG OF BLOATATION ....Drunk

LAMESTAIN .... Uncool person

TOM-TOM CLUB .... Uncool outsiders

ROCK ON .... A happy goodbye

OYSTERS OF NOTE

KUMAMOTO
Crassostrea sikamea

The local favorite originally from Japan is a good starter oyster, thanks to its buttery—rather than briny—punch on the palate.

OLYMPIA
Ostrea lurida

The West Coast's only native oyster. Small in size but big on flavor: pungent and sweet with a distinctly coppery aftertaste.

PACIFIC
Crassostrea gigas

The most ubiquitous oyster in the state hails from Japan and flaunts crowd-pleasing, flavorful meat with notes of cucumber and melon.

THE VIRGINICA
Crassostrea virginica

An Eastern Seaboard native but a Washington shores staple, this bivalve is plump and briny and served at the best seafood spots in town.

1962 WORLD'S FAIR

Life
February 9, 1961

The Northwest's biggest city is stirring with the same fever that had gripped it in 1909 when the Alaska-Yukon-Pacific Exposition helped put Seattle on the map. Near the center of town is rising a gateway into the future—the 1962 Seattle World's Fair. Pegged to a space-age theme, the fair is a spectacular reach to new horizons and a lusty expression of the country's faith in getting there. … On April 21, it will be opened by President Kennedy. … Dominating the grounds will be a towering Space Needle and the highly futuristic Coliseum Century 21. There will be science displays, art shows and concerts. But the fair will also harken back to the high spirits of frontier times with horse shows, circuses and puppet acts and a freewheeling girlie extravaganza.

"NEGRO LABOR AT BOEINGS"

The Northwest Enterprise
March 8, 1940

The Boeing Airplane Company is aided by the Aeronautical Mechanics Union in its discrimination policy, it was learned this week. Proof that the union is unanimously in accord with the Company's policy was established when it was learned that members of the union are required to take the following pledge; "I will not recommend for membership in this union any other than members of the white race." … Efforts to break down the Boeing Company's discrimination policy were made last October when young Race men applied for training at the Boeing shops following the launching of a program to train additional men to fill the company's back orders. However, Negroes were told at the plant that the company did not train nor hire Negroes. … The Boeing Airplane Company was awarded a contract of $8,102,892 in September of 1939 by the War Department for bombardment planes and also had at that time a $300,000 contract to supply the Brazilian Air Corps with training planes.

Black community newspaper The Northwest Enterprise *campaigned to integrate Boeing's Seattle factories. In 1942, stenographer Florise Spearman and sheet metal worker Dorothy West Williams became the air giant's first Black employees.*

"BRUCE LEE, KUNG-FU IDOL, LAID TO REST"

The 180 persons invited to yesterday's services included his relatives, friends, former kung-fu pupils [Lee had taught the martial arts in Seattle and California] and business associates. Also present were Steve McQueen and James Coburn, actors, both former kung-fu students of Lee's. They were among the six pallbearers carrying Lee's casket to its gravesite at Lake View Cemetery ... Lee's body was attired in the navy-blue tunic he wore during the filming of "Fists of Fury," the film that catapulted him to become Southeast Asia's "first superstar ... the new James Bond." ... Eulogies for Lee were delivered by Taky Kimura, the Seattle grocer Lee had called "my No. 1 friend;" Ted Ashley, chairman of the board of Warner Brothers, and Lee's wife. Warner Brothers will handle distribution in this country of the kung-fu expert's last picture, "Enter the Dragon." *Esquire* magazine has predicted the film, due to be released in a few weeks, would make Lee "the most famous martial artist in America, as he is in much of the rest of the world." ... Coburn delivered a short farewell: "Farewell brother. It has been an honor to share this space in time with you. As a teacher and as a friend you brought my physical being together. Thank you and peace be with you." —*The Seattle Times, July* 31, 1973

KENNY G

Few Seattle luminaries divide opinion like this crinkle-haired smooth sax player.
Yet G. is an institution: 75 million-plus sales, 17 Grammy noms,
an annual multiday hometown gig.

1956 .... Kenneth Gorelick born in Seattle. Grows up in Seward Park.
1966 .... Begins studying saxophone, a Buffet Crampon alto
1973 .... Turns pro as a sideman for the eminent Barry White
1970s ...... Member of prominent funk-soul band Cold, Bold & Together
1982 .... Arista Records solo debut, backed by ace keyboardist Jeff Lorber
1986 .... "Songbird" released. Ultimately hits no. 3 on the *Billboard* Adult
          Contemporary chart
1990s ...... Salad days: *The Bodyguard, Breathless,* World Cup anthem gig
1997 .... 45-minute hold on E flat demonstrates circular breathing prowess
2009 .... Weezer collab baffles observers, not to mention parties involved
2014 .... Hong Kong protest sympathies ruffle Chinese government

GREAT FIRE

"Not Much Of Seattle Left"
The New York Times
June 8, 1889

SEATTLE, Washington, June 7—Words almost fail to describe the awful picture painted by the fire. It is Chicago repeated on a smaller scale, and this city will arise from her ashes, too. It is now estimated that the total loss to the city, in buildings alone, is ten millions, and all personal losses will probably reach twenty millions. It is feared that many persons perished. Every bank, hotel, and place of amusement, all the leading business houses, all newspaper offices, railroad stations, miles of steamboat wharves, coal bunkers, freight warehouses, and telegraph offices were burned. The fire began at 2:30 P.M., and before midnight it had consumed the whole of the business section of the city. The city is literally wiped out ... Valiantly did the Fire Department fight the fire, but without avail.

> *Ignited by an upset glue bucket in a carpenter's shop, the fire wiped out the wooden pioneer town. Rebuilding spurred a population boom.*

OCTOPUS WRESTLING

The octopus must be captured by hand. It may not be mauled, mutilated or penetrated in any manner. Gloves and knives may be worn, but no firearms may be carried ... Teams must present evidence of previous octopus-wrestling experience, because this is a somewhat dangerous event. The entries will include Jack Myers, already the unofficial claimant to the world's octopus-wrestling championship, skin-diving division [he nabbed a 9-footer once], Joe Dollinger and Walt Mackey of Seattle's Beachcomber Club [who played it doubles and got an 18-footer while lung-diving], Tom Ammerman, Portland [best catch, a 125-pounder, lung-diving], and Jim Blanchard and [John] Tallman. ... Gary Keffler, another Mudshark, also will try his hand on octopus, after having run out of Pacific Northwest competition in the wrestling of ling, a big, bellicose cod.
—*The Seattle Sunday Times, March 10, 1957*

INTERNMENT

Letter from 19-year-old Kenji Okuda to friend Norio Higano describing Camp Harmony, in the Seattle suburb of Puyallup, May 12, 1942.

Dear Norio,

Here I am, and I've been for almost the last two weeks, sitting on my haunches in the "assembly center"—what a name—at Puyallup watching the days roll by. Hell, what a feeling! Cooped in by fence with armed guards patrolling outside and submachine guns in the watch towers, powerful search lights playing in the area between the barracks and the fence, watched by armed guards the moment we leave to go to another camp—what a mess!

Thanks for the two letters, the last one of encouragement. And I apologize for the delay, but I've been quite busy until now. You've probably got the physical details of the camp from your sis, but I'll explain as best I can and hope that you can get a good idea of what is happening here....

The Puyallup assembly center is divided, as I explained before, into four areas, A, B, C, and D. We're in A in the northeast corner of the fairgrounds. At present the population of this area "A" is about 2,500 or 2,600, and I've just heard tonight that a group from Tacoma might be put into this section. I wouldn't mind that at all—not at all! The whole population is accommodated by 23 rows of barracks with 4 barracks in each row running north and south with 7 rooms, apts., or boxes in each long building. ... Between groups of two avenues are the "cans" and showers ... one of each for the men and women. They aren't bad, but the water just seems to refuse to run the correct way, and we have the makings of a second flood. But we ditch diggers are doing our best to remedy the mess. There isn't any privacy in both the "cans" and showers, but when nature calls, who in the H cares. I prefer to call this place Camp "H" instead of Camp Harmony....

It is now 10 p.m., and so I must turn off the lights and hit the hay. I will carry on again tomorrow.

Two months after Pearl Harbor, Franklin D. Roosevelt's Executive Order 9066 forced the West Coast's Japanese Americans into internment camps. That included some 7,000 Seattleites. In the city's bustling Japantown, storefronts, especially on Jackson Street, emptied overnight and remained shuttered throughout the war.

GENERAL STRIKE

Seattle Union Record, February 3, 1919

"SIXTY THOUSAND RESPOND TO CALL"

At 10 o'clock next Thursday morning 60,000 organized workers in the city of Seattle will stand shoulder to shoulder in the first general strike that has ever been successfully inaugurated in the history of this country. Insolently and contemptuously Mr. Charles Piez and his labor-snubbing shipping board threw down the defiant gauntlet which has now been taken up with a firmness of resolution and a solidarity unmatched in the annals of the American labor movement. The workers of the northwest believe that they have been flouted and fooled by Piez and his fellow labor-baiters, that they have been deceived and betrayed by the politicians, both state and federal, and they have resolutely grasped the only weapon over which they have any direct control, determined to make a fight that will demonstrate whether or not they have the power to secure the justice that has been denied them by industrial barons and bureaucratic despots.

> *Sparked by Great War wage controls and involving more than 100 unions, the Seattle General Strike lasted from February 6 to 11, 1919. Workers distributed food and maintained public order. Lacking clear goals, the strike dissipated, but still shapes Seattle's political traditions to this day. The poem below appeared in the* Union-Record *on February 8.*

"They Can't Understand"
By Anise [aka Anna Louise Strong]

What scares them most is
That NOTHING HAPPENS!
They are ready
For DISTURBANCES
They have machine guns
And soldiers.
But this SMILING SILENCE
Is uncanny.
The business men
Don't understand
That sort of weapon

VESSELS OF NOTE

Virginia V	Last of the "mosquito fleet" that linked city, islands. Steam-powered, old-growth-built, 1922.
USCGC Polar Star	America's only heavy icebreaker deploys on Antarctic rescue missions.
Halibut Schooners	A handful of antique wooden fishing vessels still sail out on working voyages.
Arthur Foss	Built in 1889: maybe the world's oldest wooden tug. Saw both Klondike and Pacific theater service.
Dixie	A hardworking tug in the Fremont fleet's signature marigold-and-white scheme.
Swiftsure	Historic Navy "lightship," now a floating museum. Built 1904, aka LV-83.
Hvalsoe 18	One of noted boatbuilder Eric Hvalsoe's solo-cruising models. Two graceful masts.
Aleutian Falcon	A 233-foot salmon-and-halibut processor exemplifies Seattle's link to northern seas.
F/V Northwestern	Crab fleet superstar helmed by Hansen family, a *Deadliest Catch* mainstay.
Pocock Racing Shells	Revered by rowers since 1912, ancestral expertise now shapes carbon-bodied models. Key to Boeing history, *Boys in the Boat* saga.
M/V Kalakala	Otherworldly art deco ferry, in service 1935-1967, sadly scrapped in 2015.
Adventuress	A century-old tall ship, now setting sail for educational missions on the Salish Sea.

For an introduction to Seattle's maritime history and superb archival photos of nautical affairs, visit the Museum of History and Industry. mohai.org

MAPS

Pictorial journeys through unique Seattle and Puget
Sound culture, commerce and landscape by local illustrator
Jordan Kay. Not to scale.

SAN JUAN

VICTORIA

PACIFIC OCEAN

OLYMPIC MOUNTAINS

FERRIES & ISLANDS

ORCAS

MT. BAKER

LOPEZ

"the PEOPLE'S FLEET"

WHIDBEY

BAINBRIDGE

SEATTLE

BREMERTON

VASHON

FERRIES & ISLANDS

The towns, cities and archipelagoes of the Salish Sea, linked by a picturesque maritime network.

WHIDBEY

A preserve of artists, postcard villages and backroads farmers, Whidbey merges Northwest fantasy and reality. Ferry: WA State Ferries, Mukilteo to Clinton *Local: Captain Whidbey Inn, Toby's Tavern, whidbeyislandgrown.com*

BAINBRIDGE

A suburb, but quite a suburb: coveted small-town life, lush gardens and forests, and a burgeoning food scene, 35 minutes from downtown. Ferry: Seattle to Bainbridge *Local: Hitchcock, Gazzam Lake Nature Preserve*

VASHON

Retirees taking up high-end cannabis farming. Experimental butchers. A tech consultant turned island poet. Vashonites all. Home of the *Beachcomber*, an all-time great newspaper name. Ferry: Fauntleroy to Vashon *Local: The Ruby Brink, Point Robinson Lighthouse*

BREMERTON

Make landfall for outdoorsy Kitsap Peninsula in a Navy town. Ferry: Seattle to Bremerton *Local: Seabeck Loop cycling*

SAN JUAN

The San Juan Islands—including San Juan itself and Orcas—dollop the sea. Galleries and shops pack Friday Harbor, this micronation's capital. Ferries: San Juan Clipper from Seattle; Anacortes to Friday Harbor *Local: Cease & Desist, Lime Kiln Point State Park*

ORCAS

Dreamy sea-village life mingles with throwback hippie vibes. Ferry: Anacortes to Orcas Island *Local: Doe Bay Resort*

VICTORIA

British Columbia's capital mixes Anglo nostalgia and Canadian crunchiness. Ferry: Victoria Clipper *Local: Empress Hotel afternoon tea, Cowichan Valley wineries*

THE PEOPLE'S FLEET *Washington State Ferries is America's largest maritime transit system, known for onboard book clubs and weddings. A plan to convert to carbon-cutting hybrid ships is underway.*

NORTHWEST OUTFITTERS

The Far Corner's adventurous heritage forged a hub for skilled outfitters, throwback gear and navigational expertise.

FIELD & STREAM

Filson

No brand captures the Cascadian ethos like this maker of waxed workwear and indestructible gear. Key supplier for range, helm or coffee meetup. Stop by the flagship to see union sewers in action and scope unique product in the Restoration Department & Workshop. *1741 1st Ave S*

NAUTICAL KNOWLEDGE

The Center for Wooden Boats

A lakeside livery offers classes and rental of vintage craft: Beetle Cats, Blanchard sailboats and Seattle-born Hvalsoe models. *1010 Valley St*

GENERAL DRY GOODS

Freeman

An American tale of a girl, a boy, an artisan raincoat design. Creators of coveted outerwear since 2011, Freeman retails spot-on neoclassic clothing brands. *713 Broadway E*

FISHING EXPEDITIONS

Emerald Water Anglers

Close-to-town Sound outings in pursuit of sea-running cutthroats. *emeraldwateranglers.com*

ALPINE AFFAIRS

The Mountaineers

This high-country society runs lodges, expeditions and classes. Its *Mountaineering: The Freedom of the Hills* sets a national standard. Members launched REI in 1930s. *7700 Sand Point Way NE*

TRADITIONAL CRAFT

Seawolf Kayak

Kiliii Yuyan adapts age-old cedar frames to modern performance expectations. *seawolfkayak.com*

OCEANIC KIT

Pacific Fishermen Shipyard

An atmospheric port of call in salty Ballard, with vintage signs and sailorly bric-a-brac, but also very real ship repair and outfitting. *5351 24th Ave NW*

WAYFINDING *Orienteering teaches navigation at speed, by map and [sometimes] compass. Cascade Orienteering Club is a training ground for youth national team competitors but welcomes newcomers. cascadeoc.org*

PACIFIC FISHERMEN SHIPYARD

SHIPYARD
DRY DOCKS
PLEASURE SHIP
REPAIRS
WELDING

MOUNTAINEERING
THE FREEDOM OF
THE HILLS

THE
MOUNTAINEERS

NORthWEST
OUTFITTERS

SEAWOLF KAYAKS

LAKE UNION

Freeman
MADE IN USA

CENTER for WOODEN BOATS

EMERALD WATER ANGLERS

FILSON

COFFEE
PHINNEY/
GREENWOOD
HERKIMER
COFFEE
LAKE
UNION
99
SEATTLE
CENTER
LA MARZOCCO
ON AIR
N

Cafe ALLEGRO

520

Analog Coffee

espresso vivace

CAPITOL HILL

Caffè

5 VIVACE SIDEWALK BAR

STARBUCKS RESERVE ROASTERY

MONORAIL ESPRESSO

ELLIOTT BAY

DOWNTOWN

COFFEE

Thanks to a certain global roaster, Seattle is synonymous with coffee.
But cafe culture here goes way beyond the omnipresent mermaid.

VIVACE SIDEWALK BAR

There's always a line at Espresso Vivace's curbside satellite, for good reason. Be sure to eye that foam. Vivace's founder invented latte art. *321 Broadway Ave E*

CAFE ALLEGRO

In operation since 1975, and one of the city's first roasteries, this former mortuary carport draws laptop-pecking university students and a surfeit of tortured poets. *4214 University Way NE*

LA MARZOCCO

KEXP's in-house coffee shop—known for exquisite pulls from the eponymous Italian espresso machine—puts you within earshot of the world-renowned station's regular live performances. *472 1st Ave N*

MONORAIL ESPRESSO

Descendent of the city's first espresso cart, which opened under the Monorail tracks in 1980, this walk-up window remains a singular Seattle coffee experience. *510 Pike St*

ANALOG

Hit this Capitol Hill exemplar of the third-wave coffee movement for no-frills calm and namesake media preferences: vinyl and newsprint. *235 Summit Ave E*

HERKIMER

No surly Seattle cool here. But affable staff are just a bonus when the by-the-bag situation is this legend. These are the beans you want to take back home. *7320 Greenwood Ave N*

STARBUCKS RESERVE ROASTERY

Often evoking comparisons to Willy Wonka's factory, this monument to all things java houses a cocktail bar, a pizzeria and a grand working roastery. Even haters gotta recognize. *1124 Pike St*

COFFEE LAB *Sebastian Simsch runs a sort of mad laboratory dedicated to drawing the best flavors from a bean. Vacuum brewing. Chemex. A 4-foot-tall, hourglass-like cold brewer. Join the experiment via daily cuppings at Seattle Coffee Works. 108 Pine St*

FISH CITY

Protein plucked from sea is Seattle's sweet spot, and so are the restaurants and markets that sell it.

RAY'S BOATHOUSE
Started in the 1930s as a Ballard boat rental shop, transformed into a fine-dining restaurant in the 1970s, remains Seattle's most iconic seafood experience. *6049 Seaview Ave NW*

SEATTLE FISH GUYS
Bona fides? The family who runs this Central District market and restaurant descends from a tackle shop owner. Pick up fresh king crab and salmon, or dine in with a salmon poke bowl. *411 23rd Ave S*

MARKET GRILL
Belly up to the old-school counter for a catch-of-the-day sandwich or herbaceous clam chowder at this Pike Place Market pillar. *1509 Pike Pl*

WESTWARD
Adirondack chairs facing the skyline and private boat docks lend this Mediterranean seafood restaurant on Lake Union the feel of a beach party. *2501 N Northlake Way*

TAYLOR SHELLFISH FARMS
One of three Seattle oyster bars run by the region's biggest shellfish harvester, this compact Capitol Hill iteration pulses with oyster-farm vibes. Vats burble with Kumamotos and Shigokus. *1521 Melrose Ave*

BAR MELUSINE
You're prepared to take your oyster bar experience up a notch. This pastel-toned gem by renown seafood restaurateur Renee Erickson is exactly the place. *1060 E Union St*

PURE FOOD FISH MARKET
Not the one with the thrown fish. Just the city's best seafood purveyor, run by the same family since 1911. They'll overnight fresh Northwest king salmon fillets. *1511 Pike Pl*

HUNT YOUR OWN *Langdon Cook, author of* Fat of the Land: Adventures of a 21st Century Forager, *offers out-in-the-wild classes on foraging and cooking clams, oysters, geoduck and more.* *langdoncook.com*

RAY'S
BOATHOUSE

BALLARD

MARKET
GRILL

MARKET GRILL

PIKE
PLACE
MARKET

FISH CITY

WESTWARD

OYSTERS!

Taylor Shellfish Farms

LAKE UNION

CAPITOL HILL

SEATTLE fish GUYS

PURE Food MARKET

BAR MELUSINE

CENTRAL DISTRICT

PURE FOOD FISH MARKET

N

OFF the REZ

JOHN T. WILLIAMS TOTEM

UNIVERSITY DISTRICT

CHIEF SEALTH STATUE

8TH GEN

PUGET SOUND

← N

NATIVE

LAKE WASHINGTON

SEATTLE·ART·MUSEUM

DOWNTOWN

DUWAMISH LONGHOUSE

CHIEF SEATTLE IS WATCHING

DUWAMISH LONGHOUSE

& CULTURAL CENTER

WEST SEATTLE

NATIVE

The Puget Sound region's original inhabitants are still here,
their influence manifest all over the city.

CHIEF SEALTH

City founders named Seattle after the Duwamish and Suquamish hereditary chief, though they Anglicized the spelling. A life-size bronze statue, unveiled in 1912—46 years after his death—honors Sealth's legacy. *2701 5th Ave*

SAM

Seattle Art Museum's permanent collection brims with Northwest Coast and Coastal Salish work, both traditional and contemporary, including sculpture, baskets, musical instruments and ceremonial masks. *1300 1st Ave*

OFF THE REZ

Food truck Off the Rez gained a brick-and-mortar outpost when the Burke Museum tapped the Native taco purveyor as its in-house cafe. Braised bison on frybread; then explore the museum's huge Indigenous collection. *4300 15th Ave NE*

DUWAMISH LONGHOUSE

The tribe that greeted white settlers in 1851 now welcomes the public to its official headquarters. In 2009, a ceremony marked the completion of the city's first new longhouse—a traditional wood-paneled gathering space—in 150 years. *4705 W Marginal Way SW*

EIGHTH GENERATION

Designer Louie Gong [Nooksack] curates Native fashion and life-style wares, including customized Vans, etched cellphone cases and challenging contemporary art on wool blankets. *93 Pike St, Ste 103*

JOHN T. WILLIAMS

In 2010, a Seattle police officer gunned down the celebrated Ditidaht First Nation carver, who held only a pocketknife and piece of wood. The event spurred police reforms. A memorial totem pole at the Seattle Center hails Williams' life and art. *305 Harrison St*

FIRST PEOPLES *The Duwamish, Muckleshoot, Puyallup, Snoqualmie,*
Suquamish and Tulalip tribes all maintain a strong presence in the city.
Coll Thrush charts the legacy and impact of these and other tribes in
Native Seattle: Histories From the Crossing-Over Place.

ARCHITECTURE

From early classicism to avant-modernism [with a bungalow obsession in between],
Seattle is marked by an aesthetic that cuts through the mist.

SEATTLE PUBLIC LIBRARY

Designed by Rem Koolhaas and Joshua Prince-Ramus, the cubistic Central Library mothership landed in 2004, saluting books and digital media. *1000 4th Ave*

....

HELIOTROPE

To match wood-sky-mountain-water panoramas, see a firm noted for restaurants and residences: exacting modernism, fused to landscape. *heliotropearchitects.com*

....

LAKE UNION HOUSEBOATS

Floating homes halo the city's most central aquatic body, blending two ideals: life aquatic and Craftsman design. Most impressive: how the abodes use limited interior space. *Eastlake, Westlake*

....

TRACY RESIDENCE

Designed by Frank Lloyd Wright, this 1955 home exhibits his vision of "Usonia," his term for the American landscape. Stone jigsawed into intricate patterns,

a sprawling one-story footprint. You know, Wright. *18971 Edgecliff Dr SW, Normandy Park*

....

SMITH TOWER

In 1914, the Smith Tower was the tallest building west of the Mississippi. Downtown skyscrapers shadow it, but its pyramid cap remains a beacon of Seattle's early innovation. *506 2nd Ave*

....

THE STUDIO HOUSE

Pitched on a hillside overlooking Puget Sound, this Tom Kundig residence is both contemporary [exposed I-beams, cement] and deceptively ersatz [using scraps from the site's previous home]. *970 NW Elford Dr*

....

BULLITT CENTER

Noted for a balanced roof arrayed with solar panels, the 2012 structure aimed to be the world's "greenest commercial building." Composting toilets, rainwater harvesting. *1501 E Madison St*

THE T SQUARE BRIGADE Shaping Seattle Architecture: A Historical Guide to the Architects, *edited by Jeffrey Karl Ochsner, brings to life people who erected today's city, from Native longhouses to mod structures.*

ISLAND

WHIDBEY

STUDIO HOUSE

HELIOTROPE

SMITH TOWER

3RD AVE

ARCHITECTURE

LAKE UNION HOUSEBOATS

BULLITT CENTER

MADISON ST.

4TH AVE.

SEATTLE PUBLIC LIBRARY

REM KOOLHAAS

THE TRACY RESIDENCE

FRANK LLOYD WRIGHT

INTERVIEWS

Sixteen conversations with locals of note about the immigrant experience, grunge origins, high-seas fishing, hospitality, arts and activism, tarot-card reading and tribal affairs

TOMO NAKAYAMA

SONGWRITER

I MOVED WITH my family to Bellevue when I was 8.

THEY BARELY SPOKE English. Always needing to adjust and improvise.

I LEARNED A lot of English from TV, MTV and radio. My first cassette tape was Wynonna.

I WAS 13 or 14 when I got my first guitar, and Nirvana was really huge. I started by learning their songs.

THERE WAS A really good all-ages music scene on the East-side. We all grew up playing in each other's bands, learning how to book shows, tour and record.

A LOT OF times my songwriting starts when I'm out walking in my neighborhood, out in the woods or out on the lakes.

WHEN ICHIRO CAME to the Mariners, that was really big. He brought an entire industry with him—all these jobs for the Japanese American community.

JAPANESE TV WOULD send all the live broadcasts to Tokyo, because people would watch every game. It would be, what, 6 in the morning over there? My job was to make sure the digital signal was working.

IT REALLY OPENED up possibilities to see someone who looked like me, who ate the same foods, not completely assimilating, but finding a place.

I'VE NEVER BEEN signed to a major label or anything. It was always just doing things on my own, making mistakes and learning from that.

I DID 14 shows in one day. I was friends with a lot of small-business owners and wanted to highlight them and bring music to unexpected places.

MY PROUDEST MOMENT was getting from Capitol Hill to Ballard in 16 minutes during rush hour.

I KNOW ALL the secret routes.

MARCELLUS TURNER

HEAD LIBRARIAN

I'VE LIVED IN cities where they were like, "Oh, the library ..." Here, I can walk down the street and someone will say, "Aren't you the library man?"

IN FOURTH GRADE, all students had to rotate through different offices in the school system. Some got the principal's office, the nurse's office, the counselor. I got the library.

I WAS CUTTING out leaves and snowflakes for the bulletin board and doing the due-date stamp.

UTICA, MISSISSIPPI. I would imagine that if it has a thousand people, that's being generous.

I GREW UP on a community college campus, so I was always surrounded by books.

MY FATHER WAS History, and my mother was Biology.

I ASK PEOPLE, "What do you want to see in your library?" Most times, they say they want us to buy a specific book.

WE HAVE PROBABLY 35 people who order books. The book is going to get ordered.

WHAT ELSE DO you want? What is the future?

ARTIFICIAL INTELLIGENCE is coming. What is that going to mean for our library system? I have seven libraries that do not have air conditioning.

I LOOK AT airports to see how they manage and move people. Airports are mini-cities—they have to do everything.

THE WAY WE are funded, libraries just aren't leaders in those arenas. So you have to watch. "Target is doing this, Target puts the self-check here. I wonder why?"

I STILL WALK through the stacks and look for books.

SOMETIMES I'll grab a chair and sit down and read the newspaper on the floor, because I'm a people-watcher, too.

MÓNICA GUZMÁN

JOURNALIST

I HAD NEVER been to Seattle. I just knew that I would love it.

I WAS WORKING for the *Post-Intelligencer*, assigned to create a whole new beat around youth, technology, this whole blog thing. This was the end of 2006, 2007.

I CAME FROM the Northeast, which is very achievement-oriented, just getting my feet wet with Seattle's culture, which wants people to be who they are.

I DON'T NEED permission to try something new? I don't need to know if it will work? I thought I needed to know that it would work.

I STARTED A publication called *The Evergrey*. It has five core values, one of which is curiosity.

YOU GO TO someone and get their story. You don't judge their story before you go and get it.

GROWING UP, I saw every movie in the world.

I WAS BORN in Mexico, but mostly grew up in New Hampshire. My first job was in a movie theater in Newington. They let us watch the movies before they came out on Fridays. I'd see four or five movies and leave at dawn.

MOVIES PUT YOU into the perspective of so many flawed characters. How can you not see yourself as a flawed character?

WHEN PEOPLE in Seattle get evidence—because we're an evidence-based culture—that we're not doing right, it's incredible how forces in the city will pull out all the stops.

YOU CAN CRITICIZE until kingdom come about whether it's effective, but people care.

WE NEED TO be the city that stands up higher than anyone else, that goes onto the streets louder than anyone else.

YOU WANT ACTION? You want bold ideas? Oh yeah, we got that.

DEAUNTÉ DAMPER

ACTIVIST

THERE HAS NEVER been an LGBTQ chair for any NAACP chapter, ever.

THIS MEANS BEING able to talk about HIV in Black churches. We put things in boxes, like HIV is just a gay man's disease. But, no, honey.

A MAGAZINE WANTED to take my picture on Capitol Hill, because I'm an openly gay man. Capitol Hill is great. It has everything when it comes to LGBTQ, but nothing when it comes to the culture of people of color.

MY COMMUNITY IS in Columbia City. You're going to take a picture of me on Rainier and Henderson.

BACK IN THE day, people thought of this place as ghetto. But there's so much heart here.

MY GRANDFATHER moved from St. Louis, my grandmother from Texas. They met at Goodwill Baptist—the most prominent civil rights church here.

MY GRANDFATHER worked at Boeing for 43 years. Built the 747, the 777, the 737.

VERY MUCH INTO church. I learned the tools I would use later in life. Finding ways to build, never sitting still. You will find a way.

I WAS ALWAYS a really open and honest child. I knew that my sexuality could never really be a conversation. So of course it was hell.

MY FATHER OWNED a tow-truck company. He started from just pennies and nickels, practically towing cars for free.

WHY WOULD YOU do something like that? My father was teaching me exactly what it looks like to show up for your community.

WHEN I WAS diagnosed, I thought my life was ending. But it just led to another space. I got back everything I thought I lost.

MY COMMUNITY, my family, my confidence.

JACK ENDINO

RECORD PRODUCER

I WAS ABSOLUTELY aware of it before anyone used the word "grunge." Basically watching this thing come into existence before my eyes, under the microscope, right in front of me.

THE AMPS DON'T matter, the mics don't matter. You can make anything work. Get people in a room, looking at each other, listening to each other and simultaneously playing in time.

LET'S TAKE WHAT we've got and make it as good as we can. Don't pin it to an artificial metronome. That has nothing to do with music. My whole point was low-budget, without being lo-fi.

FROM THE VERY first jams of my very first band, I had microphones in the room. If you didn't have a recording, you couldn't prove that anything happened.

IT'S LIKE I needed to record to make myself believe I was actually a musician. As things got better, that got more believeable.

PEOPLE SAID, "Well, hey, can you record us?" I started doing basement jobs for $5 an hour.

I BECAME PARTNERS with Chris Hanzsek, the guy who released *Deep Six*, a compilation of early Seattle grunge bands. We started as Reciprocal Recording in the summer of 1986.

THE AMBITION WAS to get a record out somehow, get in the van and start playing shows in other cities, no matter what it takes.

THERE WAS A general intent to rock out. A general disdain for anything pretentious. People wanted to be informal and express violent, exuberant energy.

I DON'T REMEMBER particular shows very well. There were three or four a week, y'know?

IN THE FALL of '86, we were working on the first Soundgarden 7-inch. That was the first time when I thought, "Wow, we've got something here."

COLLECTIVELY, they were blindingly good players. They had a secret weapon in Chris Cornell.

....

BY LATE 1986, people were starting to talk about it. By '87, we knew something was going on.

....

WE DIDN'T KNOW the rest of the world would catch on.

....

IT'S PARTLY the weather, which is terrible most of the time. It may have something to do with the fact that psychedelic mushrooms grow wild around here.

....

BLEACH WAS FOUR or five evenings, basically—maybe 30 hours. Which only works if you have a band that's very prepared.

....

NICE GUYS from the sticks, basically. Not Seattle people.

....

NIRVANA'S SONGS WEREN'T quite as catchy initially, but everyone knew the singer had something going on.

....

KURT WOULD SAY, "Wait a minute, I have to finish the lyrics." He would sit and finish the lyrics and say, "OK, I'm ready." Just like that. He'd been singing something repetitive, or gibberish, maybe. No one realized it.

....

PEOPLE DON'T GO into the studio passed out or drunk or whatever. They're not stupid. They're excited to make a record.

....

RECORDS THAT ARE not overly produced tend to stand the test of time. I would refer you to the Creedence records as Exhibit A.

....

MUDHONEY sounds amazing the way they are. You don't fuck with that. They don't get too far from the basic ingredients.

....

IT JUST KEPT escalating. At a certain point, it escaped me. I kept going with my own bands, which fortunately avoided any sort of stardom scenario.

....

THERE'S SOME ambivalence, because frankly it didn't prove to be very good for a lot of people's health, if I can be euphemistic.

....

THE STORY ARC is tough, even going right up to a few years ago when Chris Cornell killed himself. It's like, really? Still?

....

PEOPLE WERE NOT psychologically prepared to be famous.

....

GRUNGE WAS OVER by 1992. Since then, there's been 500 more records I've worked on.

....

THERE ARE A lot of people who are still making great records.

....

I'M IN FOUR bands right now.

LIZ KANG YATES

SHOP OWNER

KIDS THINK WE'RE a candy store. Their little faces are always pressed against our windows. I'm saying, "Yeah, drag your moms in!"

K BANANA IS a place to discover new beauty products out of Korea. Whatever is trending, we want to be one of the first places that you can try it, smell it, test it.

BOTH MY PARENTS are Korean. Growing up, we'd go there for extended periods, a month or so.

WE STARTED SEEING so much innovation, whether it's using snail mucin or older products like ginseng mixed with ginger.

KOREAN PACKAGING, stationery, food. Everything is so cute.

WE WOULD WONDER why we didn't have that in the States. Finally, I thought, "Well, what if I created a space?"

MY DAD CAME here as a college student. Then my mom joined him. It's just amazing to me. English is not your first language. Halfway around the world and raising three daughters.

MY MOM TAUGHT Korean language school every Saturday, and I did it from 5 years old till I graduated high school.

ALL THE BEST Saturday morning cartoons are on, and you're making me go to school?

THE CITY HAS changed so much. On the good side, it brings in different people, new restaurants, things like that.

BUT THE CITY is so expensive. It's so hard to afford any type of housing.

I LOVE HAVING four seasons. Being able to go from ocean to mountains. There are hikes in the city, and hikes an easy 15 minutes away.

I SNOWBOARD, rock climb, hike, bike, all that stuff. I'm a Northwesterner.

NORM STAMPER

FORMER POLICE CHIEF

I GREW UP in National City, California, a Navy town. It had a significant Latino population and a lot of segregation.

WHICH SIDE OF the tracks do you live on? Or really, which side of National Boulevard?

I HAD LIMITED but unhappy experiences with cops. Then I became one.

SAN DIEGO IS a sprawling California city with freeways crisscrossing it. Seattle is kind of an East Coast city in some respects.

POLICING IS hidebound. Traditional. By definition, it's paramilitary, bureaucratic, top-down. Very masculine. It has enormous power, especially at the neighborhood level.

WE DID TENS of thousands of hours of planning for WTO. All essentially ineffective. We were outnumbered, outplanned, outsmarted. And when I say we, I mean me.

I REMEMBER, at the peak of the clash, seeing half a dozen horses wearing face shields and thinking "Well, my god."

I MADE THE worst decision of my career on the second day.

A HUGE CROWD of protesters sat and occupied an intersection.

IT WAS A key intersection. Right outside the Sheraton, a block or so away from the convention center. WTO ministers were threatened with being trapped.

WHAT IF SOMEONE is bleeding out on the other side? Or giving birth on the 27th floor of the Sheraton?

TEAR GAS, AGAINST nonviolent fellow Americans.

THEY HAD VIOLATED the public-safety right of the police to say, "Fine, protest, but you can't have this intersection."

TODAY, I WOULD say, Why not?

JODY HALL

ENTREPRENEUR

I WAS ONE of those crazy people who got married after college, right after my 22nd birthday.

I DON'T THINK I knew I was gay.

WE BOUGHT A house in Tacoma. It was coming time for Christmas. I was like, "Oh my gosh, we're broke. I'm going to moonlight at Starbucks."

THEY WERE IN Seattle, Portland, Vancouver, BC, and they had just opened in Chicago.

HOWARD SCHULTZ HAD this idea around espresso, and around gathering. Going to Italy, seeing people at bars and cafes.

THEY ASKED ME to come on board full time. Great. I don't want to work a stupid finance job downtown.

HOWARD WOULD SAY, "We're in chapter one of a 50-chapter book. We are going to change the world. We need to solve problems and not get too distracted."

THINGS I LOVED about Starbucks culture still live within me.

MAN, BEING HEARD is pretty beautiful.

NEVER DESTROY self-esteem. Say, "Wow, great idea. I hadn't thought about that."

ASK FOR HELP. We're all figuring out this massive puzzle: how we're going to scale.

YOU COULD SAY you didn't understand something and not feel ashamed about that.

I WAS JUST coming out as a lesbian, getting divorced. And I said, "The cover of *Time* called Sarah McLachlan and Natalie Merchant coffeehouse pop. We should sponsor Lilith Fair."

AFTER WE LAUNCHED Cupcake Royale in 2003, I sat down with Howard. "Howard, now that I'm the entrepreneur, I want to know your best lesson." He said, "Take care of your people."

LINDA DERSCHANG

TAVERN OWNER

WHAT'S THE MAGIC recipe? I don't know. How do you write a hit song?

I OPENED MY first business in 1984, a punk-rock clothing store.

YOU DIDN'T call yourself a "creative." You were an artist, or you weren't.

I WOULD GO to New York three times a year. People would say, "Why did you not move to New York? Or LA? Why Seattle?"

BY 1990, those same people were saying, "How did you know?"

LANDLORDS THOUGHT YOU were going to build a bar, go out of business, and what would they do with the space?

I CALLED THIS guy up, Ming Conrad. He drove me around, showed me a few places. He pulled up in front of this Middle Eastern restaurant, the Ali Baba.

I SAID, "Oh, my God, the address is 707. That's my lucky number." I'm sure he thought, Who is this nut?

WE GUTTED THE place and opened in February of 1994.

WE USED AN old cabinet from a drugstore in Pioneer Square. We used salvaged wood, old paintings, wagon-wheel lamps from my friend's vintage store, taxidermy.

IT WASN'T COMMON then, and it wasn't that I was so advanced. I just liked old stuff.

YOU CAN'T SAY, "I'm going to open an institution." The neighborhood has to choose you.

I WAS RECENTLY at a flea market at New York, and a woman had these little ceramic pieces: a 1930s sailor, and a sea captain with a pipe in his mouth. I was just getting the captain.

SHE SAYS, "It breaks my heart that they wouldn't be together."

ABSOLUTELY. I'm taking both of them.

WALTER MCQUILLEN

COMMERCIAL FISHERMAN

I STARTED IN 1980, the day after I graduated from high school: salmon fishing, trolling off Washington and Oregon. Then I moved up to Alaska and kind of slid into long-lining.

WE GOT THESE miles of rope, basically. With black cod fishing, we've got a hook every 39 inches, and we're hand-baiting all those. Fifteen thousand hooks a day or something like that.

MOSTLY IT'S HERRING, but we've been using pollock lately and some squid. We're going to get 10,000 pounds of herring, all chopped up into little pieces, and we put them on the little hook.

IT TAKES US three days to get up to Ketchikan, then another three, four days up to Yakutat.

YOU MAY SEE the outline of some mountains, or you might not see anything.

THE MAKAHS CAUGHT a lot of halibut. We were whalers, and we still are. We're people of the water.

I WAS HANGING out in Ballard in the mid- to late '80s, when I was single, when it wasn't so gentrified yet.

YOU WERE SERIOUS about your drinking if you went down to Ballard Avenue. There was a place that opened at 6 a.m., with vodka and water for $1.

MOST OF US are family men now, who happen to leave for work five, six months of the year.

THE WEATHER CAN be so nasty. I was on a boat, a wave blew out some windows. Who in their right mind would fix the windows just to get back out there?

OFF CAPE SAINT Elias, it was blowing over 100 for three days.

I'VE KNOWN PEOPLE that aren't here anymore because they just didn't keep the water out of the boat for some reason.

HOPEFULLY YOU GET a decent trip and come back to town. I don't know why it's so addictive.

GREG LUNDGREN

MUSEUM FOUNDER

SEATTLE WAS STARTED by prospectors. People came to the Pacific Northwest and said, "I'm going to make a fortune here."

WE HAVE ALL the ingredients: wealth, creative community, technology. Like if you're going to make the best chocolate chip cookie in the world.

FOR SOME REASON, Seattle hasn't mixed them in the right proportions. I think that's what has kept me here.

THE TWO WEALTHIEST men in the history of the world live here. We have 13 multi-billionaires within 10 miles.

MUSEUM OF MUSEUMS was a reaction to frustration. Big money doesn't think our city is worth celebrating.

IF A DERELICT building is for lease, it's a narrow window to decide the next 50 or 100 years.

THIS BRILLIANT three-story, midcentury medical building, boarded up. Vandalized. It had 3 tons of squatter trash inside. It had 26 broken windows.

EIGHT THOUSAND square feet: We're occupying every inch. It's designed to create opportunities for regional artists. And to show visitors we are a formidable city.

I WAS SENDING letters to General Motors when I was 8 years old, with catalytic converters I thought would make cars emit zero exhaust. I have the rejection letters.

MY FATHER WAS a lawyer, my mother was an English-as-a-second-language teacher. I think they looked at me with curious eyes. "What is this? Who is this person we created?"

I'M TOO INVESTED to stop. So it's going forward, whether it's going off a cliff or on a long-distance run.

THE MOMENT I think Seattle is incapable of creating a Renaissance, I'm out, I'm done.

KATE WALLICH

CHOREOGRAPHER

PEOPLE ASK, "WHAT'S Dance Church?" It's easier to say, look at this picture. A photo of a girl staring at the beach. That's Dance Church.

IT'S AN ALL-LEVELS movement class. It has a club mentality. It's a really good workout, if you're into that.

I GREW UP in Tecumseh, Michigan. Kids played football and soccer. Show choir. But I started dancing at the age of 3.

I WAS AT the studio from 3:30 until 9 p.m. An obsessed middle-schooler in love with dance.

I WAS THE one kid doing a solo competition dance to a Metallica song, wearing all black.

MY DAD'S grandfather started Wallich Lumber. The original models in the Henry Ford Museum have signs that say "Lumber courtesy Wallich Lumber."

I'M THE DAUGHTER of an educator and an entrepreneur.

I HAD A mentor at Cornish, Tonya Lockyer. She gave me the keys to her studio space in Pioneer Square.

I WAS WORKING at a coffee shop. I didn't have money to go and audition for jobs in New York. I also didn't have the fire under my ass to do that.

I FELL IN love with a woman— I had always considered myself straight. My brother got really sick. There was a lot going on.

THE STUDIO REALLY became a place to take that tension and anger in my body and filter it out into something I found beautiful.

WHEN I STARTED Dance Church, it was five of us in a room.

THAT GREW TO 20 people, to 25, to 30, to 40. All of a sudden it went to 80. From five people to 220 at a megachurch.

I ALWAYS SAY, feel your heartbeat, and the heartbeats of the

people around you. That's powerful: to consider yourself, but also to consider others.

....

IT'S NOT JUST about the expe-rience of the class. It's about how you went to the class. What happens before and after class.

....

THAT'S WHAT RITUAL is, right?

MARK CANLIS

RESTAURATEUR

CANLIS IS ON a busy road, a mile outside of downtown.

WE GREET YOU at the door.

YOU DON'T KNOW but we've parked your car and memorized who you are. Same thing with your coat. Hopefully you don't notice that either.

LOOK AT THE beginning of hospitality, three or four thousand years ago.

PEOPLE TRAVEL from one place to another, and eventually they run out of daylight, maybe they run out of water or food. They become vulnerable. They're smelly, needy, likely armed.

THERE'S A KNOCK at the door.

THE HOUSE ON the outside of town. This is the beginning of hotels and restaurants.

WE WANT OUR guests to feel that it's safe here, that they can trust this place.

I CAN'T EXPECT my staff to give away what I'm not giving them.

WHEN I HIRE someone, I ask them: If you're going to work here, we're going to put you through a crucible. How do you want to grow?

LIKE WHO CARES? It's just dinner. But who are you hoping to become at Canlis? What if we got to be a part of that?

HOSPITALITY THE WORD, in Latin, means to make space for the stranger.

WE DON'T KNOW until we meet you where you're going to sit. We build the dining room each night, like putting logs on a fire.

THE FOOD AND wine and the service are as good as anywhere in America. But that's not what sets Canlis apart.

YOU COME IN the night before your wife has a baby. Your first anniversary. You bring in your grandma who's suffering from cancer.

YOU PAY ME a ton of money for dinner, but really what's being spent here are once-in-a-lifetime opportunities.

YOU NEVER get that night back.

WE BOUGHT THE company from my parents in 2007.

I HAD BEEN in New York running a restaurant for Danny Meyer. My brother Brian was in the Air Force.

MY great-grandparents came over from Greece and Lebanon. They opened a restaurant in California in 1908. Their son, my grandfather Peter, founded Canlis [Seattle] in 1950.

SOME OF THAT legacy looks more like a curse than a blessing.

HE WAS A genius, but also a train wreck. Alcoholic, married no one knows how many times.

HE LUCKED INTO this spot. He wanted to be downtown, but this guy told him, "I have a piece of property outside of town."

PETER SAID, "WITHIN a dollar cab ride to the city?" It was.

THE ARCHITECT Roland Terry designed Canlis to feel like a home.

He hired all these artists to come build it out. Like George Tsutakawa, the Northwest sculptor who is famous here—our door handle was his very first sculpture.

THE NORTHWEST was still becoming itself in the 1950s. Being so strongly shaped by Asia—what a gift.

WHEN PEOPLE LEARN you're a 70-year-old restaurant, they envision old men, old tuxedos, a 70-year-old salad.

A RESTAURANT IS a living, breathing thing. Our chef Brady Williams joined us five years ago. He is hugely influential in all we do. We would not be here without him.

WE'RE CREATED TO come together and eat. It's what we do at the highest moment.

YOU'LL FEEL MORE comfortable at Canlis that you ever dreamed you would. The stuff we bring you, those are just distractions. What's happening, slowly, is that we're getting to know you.

IT'S AN ENDLESS source of wonder. There's so much to learn, from one another, from this celebration.

THE FEELING IS like, "I needed that." You walk out feeling restored.

JOHN RICHARDS

DISC JOCKEY

MY BIG BROTHER moved from Spokane to Seattle. He'd send me music. To me, it might as well have been another planet.

I WAS WORKING a night job, stocking shelves. I got in my car at the end of the shift and drove all the way across the state. Knocked on his door, just like, "If I moved here, could I stay here?"

KCMU IS WHAT became KEXP.

I JUST KEPT showing up. I alphabetized the entire vinyl library. I would never leave. Eventually, they had to give me a shift.

THE 1 TO *6* a.m. shift, on Friday. Great. I was available.

KCMU WAS STARTING to implode. Then, all of a sudden, there's this billionaire, Paul Allen, hanging out, wanting to work with the station. Like, that's most likely going to go a bad way.

MY BROTHER SAID, "What if it's good?" No one had said that yet.

OUR GOAL WAS to make KEXP a brand that meant independence, music and community. People thought we were insane.

I KNEW THE other lazy DJs wouldn't apply for the morning show. I was right. If you're a DJ you want to be on in the morning. You want to be in the foreground.

I BECAME BETTER on the mic after my father passed. He died on a Saturday, and I was on the air that night.

I SAID, "HEY, my dad died. I'm on the air. I'm going to play songs that are going to make me feel better. If you're out there, I hope this helps you."

IT WAS THE most response I'd ever gotten.

YOU DON'T WANT to plan too much. You want to flow.

I CAN'T REMEMBER my kids' birthday, but I remember every song ever made. I admit to that.

XTINA

TAROT READER

THE WHOLE POINT of what I do is to hold up a mirror.

I DON'T TALK to dead people.

I GET ATTACHED to my decks. I really like the Aquatic. I never vibed with the Thoth, the Aleister Crowley deck.

I WAS USING the Wild Unknown, a beautiful deck. And then it just stopped speaking to me.

I STARTED COMING to Pike Place Market in the mid- to late '80s. I was living in the Midwest, but my dad lived here. I would come out to Seattle and be like, "I have to go to the Market."

TENZING MOMO IS an apothecary, a perfumery. It was my favorite store as a teenager, before I knew I'd end up there decades later.

MY DAUGHTER GREW up in the Market. I was totally fine with her running around. She knew every nook and cranny.

IT'S LIKE A beehive.

MY FAVORITE DAYS at the Market are offseason, rainy. You know half the people there.

OR A REALLY good day would be walking to work, saying hi to my friend who owns the lavender stand, grabbing coffee at Crêpe de France. Maybe I'll get a cup of soup at DeLaurenti.

PEOPLE LIVE AT the Market. There are tons of apartments, an old folks' home.

MY LEAST FAVORITE card is the Five of Cups. It often represents disappointment.

THERE'S A CARD that to me has a phoenix energy.

SEATTLE BURNS DOWN and rises up, burns down, rises up.

IN THE '70S, someone made a sign that said, "The last person in Seattle, turn out the lights." Ten years later, Microsoft.

I FEEL LIKE Seattle has the phoenix energy.

CECILE HANSEN

TRIBAL CHAIR

I WAS TRYING to make a berry cobbler. I got the crust together, so I can set that aside.

MY BROTHER WAS fishing in the Duwamish River. One day, he got cited by the fisheries people. And of course our position is, if you're Duwamish, you can fish in the Duwamish River.

HE SAID, "YOU got to get involved. You just have to go to a few meetings." That's 1974.

IN THE SPRING of '75, I was elected chair. Clueless, very clueless.

I'M GETTING UP there. But the deal is, I don't want to throw in the towel, because what I've been fighting for us is the rightful status of the Duwamish Tribe.

THE LAST DAY of the Clinton administration, I got a call from someone saying, you're recognized.

THE FOLLOWING MONDAY, we got a fax saying that the decision was put on hold. So we've been appealing that since 2001.

WHEN WE SIGNED the treaty, settlers burned down all the longhouses along the riverways.

MY PARENTS WERE Native, but we're urban Indians. I was never taught any language.

WE GAVE UP 54,000 acres. Fifteen years ago, we bought property, and we own two-thirds of an acre. I call it our little mini-rez.

THE WHOLE POINT of our longhouse is to educate the city.

IT'S CALLED REAL Rent. Thousands of people pay us "rent," because they honor us.

WE OPENED IN 2009. And I have not had one mayor come and meet with me.

I AM THE great-, great-, great-niece to Chief Sealth [Si'ahl] on my mother's side. You've got to honor the chief. They named a city after him.

YOU CAN'T SAY we're not here, because we're here. You know?

STORIES

---

*Essays and selected writing from
noted Seattle voices*

LET SEATTLE BE

Written by **JOURDAN IMANI KEITH**

Let Seattle be
      Seattle, the place that was, and is, and will be
      Seattle has become a home for me
      among the shackled and the free

The place where trees once stood
      before there was a neighborhood
      Seattle was the Cedar's majesty
      before the planes and glass spines scraped the sky
      she was the mother in her children's eyes
      before the hills were pushed into the sand
this was and is and will be the Duwamish land

See the last one leaving turn out the lights
See the home of War and the flight
See the Gold Rush and sourdough bread
See the Issei and the Nisei of the Panama Hotel, 7,000 gone by
      what the president said

Say, who are you in the Salish Sea?
      Pushed aside for prosperity
I am the Black River gone as the people cried
I am the Chinook dead on the side
I am the Orca carrying my child
I'm the gray whale beached at Alki
I am your neighbor
             without shelter in the sand

Oh, but Seattle is mighty even with its broken dreams
Oh, Seattle is mighty when it looks in its own eyes
What city do you know that fights itself to undo its present harms
What city do you know that sounds its own alarms?
What city do you know that was raised by colonizers
that turns itself upon itself to put out ancient fires?

This place, of wooded paths and parks
                                    that must belong to all
This place, where we drink the water from protected Cedar Falls
This place, where race and social justice is built into the law
This place, where you are taught to understand the power of it all
The power of illusion that there are racial lines
The power of Illusion that's kept us all behind
But the strength of our ethnicity is celebrated here, So

Sing what's right Seattle
          over the heartless song
Sing the estuary where freshwater meets the sea
          where Orcas must survive for our health and their dignity
Sing My Posse's on Broadway
Sing jazz on Jackson Street in wires
Sing Jimi Hendrix, what stars is in his Spangled Banner demand
Sing WTO, Black Panthers and the Women's March
Sing an Endangered song, Sing a whale's song, Sing
Sing Quincy Jones
Sing Ernestine Anderson
Sing Grunge and Hip Hop
Speak Octavia Butler and her brood in a futuristic mood
Dance/color into the dark canvas of Winter
Dance Chihuly in two steps
Dance Jacob Lawrence and Debora Moore
Become an Amazon for equity
with the sweet steamy foam of justice in our mouths —

SING WHAT's RIGHT SEATTLE

Let Seattle be
      Seattle, the place that was and is and will be
Seattle has become a home for me
      among the shackled and the free
      amidst the resistance there must be
      as the hills were pushed into the sand
Seattle will bring
      must bring
            Justice to our land

JOURDAN IMANI KEITH is a storyteller, essayist, playwright, naturalist, activist and the City of Seattle's 2019–2021 Civic Poet. Her TEDx Talk, "Your Body of Water," the theme for King County's 2016–2018 Poetry on Buses program, won an Americans for the Arts award. Her memoir in essays, *Tugging at the Web*, is forthcoming from University of Washington Press.

FERRIES

Written by **BROOKE JARVIS**

I HAD READ, in the ad for my new job, that the place I was moving to was an island, with great hiking trails, "off the coast of Seattle." Having never been to Seattle or, I guess, looked properly at a map, I took this snippet of information and with it conjured a vision: The island would be small and forested, far off the coast, sitting alone in a choppy sea. It would not have any cars on it. The people would live in cottages and come and go by, well, I wasn't sure exactly. Foot and bicycle, certainly. Maybe also…funiculars? I had to take a ferry to get there, so any sort of strange wonder might be possible.

I grew up in Tennessee, on the rolling edge of mountains. At 22, I had taken a ferry just once, to camp under 600-year-old live oaks on a sea island off the coast of Georgia. [When we missed the boat we meant to catch, we had to pitch tents next to a gas station and await the next day's sailing.] To actually make your life at the far end of a ferry ride sounded like inhabiting an old movie or a children's book, like living somewhere just slightly beyond the edges of the normal world.

I took a couple of planes, a shuttle, and walked eight steep blocks through downtown Seattle to the waterfront. The ferry that greeted me was painted green and white, with trim railings and smokestacks that looked an extremely tiny bit like the RMS *Queen Mary*'s. It was enormous, with a gaping mouth where the cars—yes, damn it, the cars—drove on and off. Together, we glided the 25 minutes to my new home on Bainbridge Island, which turned out to have traffic and condos and commuters and a McDonald's drive-thru and all the rest of it. [It also, oops, turned out to be a mountain range away from the Pacific Ocean, in a far less imposing body of water that suddenly clicked into place in my mental map: oh right, the Puget Sound.] You could even drive right off the other side of the island. On a bridge!

But still, that ferry. It navigated the regular world, but never seemed to be quite of it. There was a sun deck from which you could look for orcas, though I never actually saw any, plus seals and eagles and the gleaming ice of distant volcanoes. There was a galley, where you could buy terrible coffee and clam chowder, and plenty of other nautical terms to encounter and feel old-timey about: muster stations and crossings, gangplanks and ordinary seamen. You could ride the ferry to Seattle just to watch the sunset, and then sail right back home again. You could ride aboard on your bicycle, whizzing alone through the ferry's enormous belly before the cars arrived. You could stand on the deck and watch a whole city appear, its buses and cranes and helicopters and skyscrapers arrayed before you like a Richard Scarry illustration. Sometimes there were jigsaw puzzles left out on the tables: joint ventures, projects passed in trust among strangers. Sometimes the ferry took you into a Sound so swathed in gray fog that you couldn't see the water beneath you—you and your fellow travelers, floating in a cabin as humid as a ski chalet, might as well be floating in space. Sometimes on summer nights you could watch the glow of tiny, bioluminescent animals churning in the darkness of your wake.

Even on land, you knew there was a ferry nearby. You could hear the foghorn bellowing in the distance, watch gulls following the ship, see the bright lights of windows like a city gliding across still water.

You could also miss the ferry, and I did. Frequently. Among my friends, I quickly became famous for missing the ferry. If there was a way to misread the schedule—switching a.m. for p.m., westward sailings for eastward ones, weekends for weekdays—then I did it. Or I just ran late, which frequently meant literal running, dead sprints down Marion Street in Seattle or Winslow Way on Bainbridge. Once, as I ran, a windowless white van rolled up beside me, and its door slid open. From inside, I heard a man's voice yell, "Get in!" And I did. Instead of a murderer, the driver was a musician, also racing for a boat he couldn't miss. I crawled in next to a bass, and we introduced ourselves only after we had made the sailing. It was a moment that only a regular ferry rider could understand.

"Missing the boat," as an idiom, isn't so distant from its origins that its real meaning is forgotten. It's not like "pleased as punch," which we now say without even a mental glance at the 17th-century Punch and Judy puppet shows from which it emerged. But in my life, it had been just a loosely tethered phrase, not evocative of any strong feelings or real experience. Not until I learned, again and again and again, what it is to stand next to a boat that you meant to be on but are unable to board. The feeling of powerlessness is complete, exquisite, overwhelming. The boat, even if it looks as though it's still right there, is gone. You are not on it.

There is not a single thing you can do about it. There is no getting where you thought you were going. You can only watch as it sails away, leaving you behind on the wrong side of the water, and think, with profound self-recrimination: "I missed the boat."

I have missed a plane because of missing the ferry on the way to the airport. I have been late for meetings, parties, concerts, dates. [Once, because fares are not collected going eastward, I failed to realize that I'd forgotten my wallet until it was too late and had to ask a first date for $8 so I could ride the ferry home at the end of the night.] I have missed the late-night boat home from the city, and endured the long, frigid wait under fluorescent lights until the very last boat leaves just after 2 in the morning. I have also missed that very last boat. I have run for the ferry in the pouring rain, then waited for the next one soaking wet. I have forced aching legs to sprint a little faster when a ferry worker yells that I might still make it. Once, after showing up for a 5:20 a.m. ferry that actually departed at 5:10, I drove my dad 90 miles, well over the speed limit, over the bridge, around the entire southern Puget Sound and north to Seattle. We had no choice, because he had a truly unmissable early morning appointment across the water: the departure of a different boat.

My original vision of life aboard ferries did not include sprinting or stress or aching frustration. The longer I have lived by the Sound, and the more I felt the indignities and inconveniences of ferry travel, the less romantic I have found the ferries. [I spent six years either on Bainbridge or in small towns on the west side of the Sound, and am now finishing my sixth in Seattle itself, a life and friendships split in two and stitched back together, just like on the maps, by ferry routes.] If you're walking aboard, the ferry's charm hits its lowest point on damp winter nights, when the wind cuts across the loading ramp; if you need to bring a car across, the nadir of the ferry experience comes on summer holiday weekends, waiting in the punishing sun as ferry after ferry with no space for you pulls away. I remember turning to a friend during one of these periods of purgatory and declaring, "This is it. This, right now, is the moment that I started to hate the ferry."

But I knew I was lying. A ferry that didn't sometimes slow you down, hinder your movements, disturb your plans would no longer be a ferry. It wouldn't be a reminder that you were crossing a body of water: an incorporate barrier, a piece of immovable geography,

unyielding to your whims and wishes because it is bigger and older and deeper than you are.

In Seattle, particularly, this felt important. The city began as a small row of houses and mills and fortifications—and, as one 1850s observer noted, "seventeen grog shops"—all squeezed onto a bit of land between a great forest and a wide tidal flat. Cut off from the mainland during high tides, and penned in by steep, unstable hills, it was an inauspicious place to build a city. But the founders chose it anyway, hoping that its deep port would offer them a profitable connection between the region's resources and the wider world of trade. This was the beginning of a long and strange relationship between the city's people and its geography. The new arrivals were attracted by nature, but only to tame and master it; they erected sawmills and dams and railroads, eventually turning their ingenuity against the city's very topography.

All cities, to some degree, buck their natural realities in order to grow. Chicago forced a river to run backward so it would carry the city's sewage away. Los Angeles and Phoenix survive on water piped over hundreds of miles. New York replaced open water and tidal flats with new land made from garbage and fill. Seattle, along with straightening its river and partially draining its great lake, did the same, but on an absurd scale. It pulled much of its new land from its old hills, using trillions of gallons of water in 60 separate projects to move millions of tons of earth into the places that planners found more advantageous. In 1909, a reporter calculated the relocated material—still only a sixth of the eventual total—would fill a train that stretched from Seattle to New York and halfway back again. The city had no patience for inconvenience, not even in the land it had chosen, and forcibly taken from its original inhabitants—people who had recognized that the sound and the lands around it were already sources of great richness. [The two groups, wrote Coll Thrush, in *Native Seattle: Histories From the Crossing-Over Place*, "spoke two mutually unintelligible languages of landscape."] In *Too High and Too Steep*, a history of Seattle's battle with its own troublesome land, David B. Williams summed up the view of the new arrivals: "Need to get from point A to point B and a hill is in the way? Lop off its top. Need better access for business? Shave away the unprofitable territory. Need flat territory for industry? Fill in the tide-flats. This was the Seattle Spirit as demonstrated through steam shovel, hydraulic giant, and dynamite."

The Sound, too, was dredged and, in its narrow places, bridged; its edges were altered and hardened; its waters polluted. But as cars and roads and speed took over everywhere, crossing the water remained an inconvenience that was never totally conquered. Instead, people adapted themselves to it, building docks and boats—so many boats, they were known as the mosquito fleet—and then ferries, public vessels that operated on their own unalterable, humility-inducing schedules. Sometimes, when the weather was rough, even they had to stay on shore.

Several years ago, a beloved friend called to say that she'd gone into labor and she wanted her friends present for the birth. Several of us had moved to Seattle, but she was on the western side of the Sound, giving birth in a farmhouse down a gravel road that carried an echo of my original vision of ferry life. There were pots of soup in the freezer, ready for the moment when a crowd would converge on the house and have an unknown time to wait.

In the city, we rushed to the ferry terminal, but a boat had just left. We waited as impatiently as I ever have, knowing that what we were missing was happening only a few unreachable miles away. Finally, a ferry came, and we raced on and off. Outside the house we heard an infant's cries and knew we were too late: The baby had arrived on her own schedule, not ours.

But there she still was, a little wonder, arrived from somewhere slightly more magical. We welcomed her into our world, with its disappointments and glories and dangers and beauties, with all the things she would want to control, and that we would want to control on her behalf, but would not be able to. She screamed and then nursed and then fell asleep, curling her tiny fingers, dreaming in her own language. We watched her for as long as we could. And then it was time to go sit and wait, again, for the ferry to come and take us home.

BROOKE JARVIS is a contributing writer to the *New York Times Magazine* and a writer for *The New Yorker* and elsewhere. She's at work on a book about insects.

GRAY

Written by **BESS LOVEJOY** | **PEOPLE WHO LIVE** elsewhere imagine that it's always raining in Seattle, but our reputation for moisture is greatly exaggerated. In fact, our average annual rainfall is less than in many East Coast cities. What it does here is drizzle, a fine mist that renders umbrellas ridiculous, and it glooms. There are many days in which the sea and sky join together into a pewter expanse with pearlescent highlights, and on certain evenings it can look as though you've crawled inside a mussel shell. Our gray is ever-present, or at least rarely far away, a blanket over the city both day and night, when the artificial light blushes the clouds a pale, grayish peach.

Unfortunately for Seattle, gray has a bad reputation. Wikipedia used to have a list of "common connotations" for gray, the first three of which were "pessimism," "depression" and "boredom." The *Oxford English Dictionary*'s definitions include the idea of something "lacking individuality," being "dull and nondescript," "lacking hope, pleasure, or cheerfulness." Gray is institutional, the dictionary tells us, the gray flannel suit "suggestive of the wearer's conservative, bureaucratic, or conformist attitude." Gray is the color not of death itself—it's not that dramatic—but of what happens afterward, cemeteries and human ashes, and the milky ends of mourning.

When I read unkind things about gray, I often wonder whether they were written by someone who knows gray intimately, someone for whom the color was a constant companion. I spent most of my childhood and adolescence across the lake from Seattle, in the suburbs of Bellevue, which in the early '90s actually did live up to the sense of gray as dull or nondescript. Seattle, by contrast, felt like a city full of mystery, where the leaden murk of the weather only encouraged a sense of depth. Some evenings, we'd drive across the I-90 floating bridge for dinner or to see art in Belltown [my former stepdad's mother is a painter] and the land would rise up from a slate-gray Lake Washington like a mirage. I was fascinated by the view of the city from that vantage point, the hills encrusted with pale houses in between the deep-green trees, and I imagined that each building held a different story. The city's topography, too, encouraged a kind of drama, each bend in the road promising another peek at the moonstone sky over the mountains.

Seattle then also symbolized all the secrets of adulthood, because in the '90s you didn't see many cool young adults in Bellevue, a place that still felt sleepy and sweetly agricultural. Once primarily berry farms and rural retreats for wealthy Seattleites, it boomed after World War II and the construction of a second bridge across Lake Washington, but the adolescent me experienced it as a featureless expanse of vinyl siding. Seattle, by contrast, felt much older, even if most of what I saw dated only to the early 20th century, and neighborhoods like Belltown—where cool nightclubs sprung up like weeds on blocks once reserved for low-income seniors—were scented with a bohemianism Bellevue would never have known how to fertilize.

My love of Seattle was also entwined with my love then of bands like Nirvana, Pearl Jam and Alice in Chains, many of whom played their first shows in Belltown at places like the Vogue Theatre, although I was far too young to attend. Their music delivered a passionate storm of sadness and rage, perfectly tuned to an adolescent's ear and heart. In the beginning, calling it grunge was uncool; that was marketing language, not preferred by the musicians themselves, but artists love to disavow the very scenes they create. "Grunge, what is that, the stuff you scrape off dishes?" a friend once said to me. But *grunge*—as opposed to broader terms like "alternative rock"—gets at the specific texture of the music, something dirty, scummy, something gray/black/brown.

Grunge is music of angst and isolation, self-annihilation—pretty rock-bottom stuff, in terms of the emotional landscape. But at its best it has the same turbulent gorgeousness as the region itself, a beauty that comes from surviving darkness. I think of being a kid watching the sun peeking through the Olympic Mountains at the end of a rainstorm, alchemizing the raindrops on a car window into diamonds.

It's this quicksilver, shape-shifting quality to gray that I think is often missed. The color has suffered at the hands of a long and distinguished line of gray haters; the artist and theorist David Batchelor, who has written extensively about gray, once called it "the slug of colours." In *Concerning the Spiritual in Art*, the artist Wassily Kandinsky writes that most colors exist in motion except for gray, which is motionless: "White is used to color pure joy and infinite purity. Black is the robe of greatest, deepest sorrow and the symbol of death. A blend of these two colors, created mechanically, produces

Grey. … Grey is, therefore, the immobility of desolation." In Ludwig Wittgenstein's *Remarks on Colour*, the philosopher sets up an opposition between "the luminous" and "the grey," writing that "whatever looks luminous does not look grey."

But that is the gray of art. It's true, the squirt of gray that comes out of a paint tube looks motionless on a flat surface, but the gray of the natural world rarely stands still. In fact, etymologists say that one of the original meanings of "gray"—it's one of our older color terms—might be "shining." Anyone familiar with a Seattle sky knows it can be luminous and gray all at once. It might be desolate, but it is often moving. Wittgenstein wrote that "We cannot conceive of something 'glowing grey,'" but when did he ever visit Seattle? [By the way, the spelling of "gray" is a gray area. Americans now spell it with an *a* and the British with an *e*, but it wasn't always so; the great British lexicographer Samuel Johnson preferred an *a*.]

A city, too, is what Batchelor calls "one of the great repositories of overlooked greys," from streetlamps to sidewalks. The grays of the urban forest are always on the move, their steel turning lighter and then darker, their concrete glimmering with dustings of mica. Seattle is a city of moody, reflective surfaces, of clouds in the skyscrapers, the Rem Koolhaas-designed Central Library, lakes Washington and Union, and even the Amazon Spheres, glass conservatories that feature plants from cloud forests across the globe. [If the tech that fueled the city's most recent booms has a color, it may be the metallic blue-gray of silicon.]

Seattle's gray is not a postindustrial gray, or what we imagine as Soviet gray: It's not block after block of the same structure dusted with coal or ash. Our grays are at play—with one another, with the light and with the green that is the city's other trademark hue. Outside downtown, in the Arboretum or one of the 37 parks designed by the Olmsted Brothers [the sons of Frederick Law Olmsted, who designed NYC's Central Park], gray often serves as a frame or accent for the giant trees covered in moss and lichen. It is nature's pearl earring.

One of the most interesting things about gray is how it is always on the verge of becoming something else, going lilac or white or black or palest blue. It is a liminal color, a hue of dawn and twilight, when the world is just making or unmaking itself. It's also a color for beings between worlds—there are at least six ghosts named the Gray Lady. Gray is also a popular color for aliens. Around half of all reported encounters in the United States describe gray aliens, according to Wikipedia, which seems like a reasonable source if we're talking about aliens. H.G. Wells may have planted the seed; his alien creatures tend to be grayish or blueish. The first modern sighting of the UFO era, by a civilian pilot named Kenneth Arnold in 1947 near Mount Rainier, didn't involve the Grays, but they were [supposedly] at Roswell later the same year, and it was the Grays who [allegedly] abducted Betty and Barney Hill in New Hampshire in 1961. Whitley Strieber's 1987 book, *Communion*, features a gray alien, and *The X-Files* had both "real" Grays and "fake" Grays, just to make things confusing.

You can see this liminality in our culture's many gray areas. While the black market is illegal, the gray market [popular during World War II rationing] is considered quasi-legal or only intermittently unethical. Black magic is meant to harm or even kill, while gray magic is more about getting what you want regardless of the ethical implications. In other cases, grayness is free of moral associations and merely means something ill-defined or interstitial. [For librarians, "gray literature" refers to written works not controlled by commercial publishers.] Gray is a color that confounds classificatory schemes, yet supports their ability to exist by providing a designated space for that which is neither black nor white.

Put another way, gray creates a safe space for complexity.

I have never been able to stay very far away from Seattle and its gray. I don't feel comfortable in places where the sun shines so brightly there's nowhere to hide. Seattle's gray encourages a kind of interiority that I value; it's possible that this is what gets mistaken for the semi-mythical "Seattle Freeze." Gray is a good color for people content to create their own worlds, whether in code or nouns and adjectives. And rather than promoting depression or annihilation, Seattle's gray has always seemed to me to encourage life—a gentle, leafy abundance that thrives in between about 40 and 70 degrees Fahrenheit. It's a temperature that doesn't require special gear or elaborate heating and cooling systems. When I first moved to Manhattan, in 2005, I was flattened by the humidity and the heat waves and dismayed to discover that in winter I needed a special weight of pants. New York's climate is actually pretty temperate, on the global scale, but I felt as though the weather was often hostile to human existence. To me, the gray in Seattle says to relax. It says to go find somewhere inside to read a good book.

After all, gray can be a balm to our hyperstimulated senses. Historically, color was expensive to produce, requiring a massacre of beetles or marine mollusks, or palaces of gems considered much more valuable than the lives used up by extracting them. The historian

Robert Finlay has written, "An individual watching color television, strolling through a supermarket, or examining a box of crayons sees a larger number of bright, saturated hues in a few moments than did most persons in a traditional society in a lifetime." Today, we could be forgiven for complaining of color exhaustion, for taking respite in the quiet dignity of gray. Gray is the opposite of Katy Perry's makeup, of tanning salons, of Florida. It's the opposite of the 24/7 news cycle, of Twitter moments and TikTok videos. It's not associated with any political party, and it doesn't want your votes.

Gray is also a modest color for a city that, at least historically, is unostentatious. Our billionaires wear khakis and sweater vests, not custom suits with diamond cuff links. We leave the gleaming gold to the White House. Gray will not bedazzle you. Our sense of beauty, like our temperament, is a little more reserved.

The Seattle love of [or at least comfort with] gray is not to suggest the elitism of Goethe, who once said, "People of refinement have a disinclination to colors." We're just embracing what we know. One of the consolatory techniques of the human brain, when all goes well, is that it learns to find beauty in what surrounds it. Art imitates life. Patterns of decoration and adornment are influenced by the natural materials, climate and flora and fauna of a place. Survey a scene of longtime Pacific Northwesterners and they are invariably clad in earth tones, driving silvery cars on silvery roads beneath a silvery sky above a silvery sea. Perhaps we are taking after the salmon, silvering our skins over pink-red insides. For us, the gray is our silver lining.

BESS LOVEJOY is the author of *Rest in Pieces: The Curious Fates of Famous Corpses*, which has been translated into three languages. Her work has appeared in *The New York Times, Lapham's Quarterly, The Boston Globe, The Public Domain Review, Atlas Obscura* and elsewhere. Her family has lived in the Puget Sound region for six generations.

REBEL CITY WALKING

Written by **KIT BAKKE** | **OAKLAND CALIFORNIA,** a typically sunny day, with a light breeze coming off the Bay. A good day for a protest rally. But not for long. Squads of well-armed police suddenly appeared—cops in khaki brown and flak vests, bristling with hand guns and tear gas canisters, leaped out of squealing unmarked cars and started to surround us. Mounted police, too, their horses always bigger and less friendly-looking than you'd like.

I spotted a convenient alley and ran down it, scattering Coke cans, candy wrappers and the odd roach clip. I was 26 years old and four months pregnant. I'd spent the previous five years working and living in the antiwar movement. Hitchhiking across the country, organizing, demonstrating, trying to right the terrible wrongs of the war in Vietnam, not to mention racism and capitalism. First I was part of SDS [Students for a Democratic Society]. Then, Weatherman and then the Weather Underground. Our tactics escalated as our names changed, becoming increasingly incendiary.

It was all far from middle-class Seattle, from my educated parents, from my expected trajectory. I grew up in a nice little neighborhood of cottages and midcentury-modern houses along Lake Washington's eastern shore. After high school there would be college, marriage and family, work and play. Nothing exciting, nothing unexpected. But by the 1960s, when I went to college, my desperate urgency to create a just world destroyed that easy path and detached me from Seattle and my parents' expectations.

As I ran down that Oakland alley, cops at my heels, I didn't know it, but I was on my way back. And about to discover a thing or two along the way.

It wasn't hard to live like my parents in the late '50s and early '60s: white, easygoing, liberal, gently progressive Democrats in Seattle. Even our Republicans were liberals. We kids grew up exploring and building forts in the woods and ravines behind our houses, or swimming and rowboating on the lake. Our dads were salesmen, seamen, Boeing engineers. Our moms stayed home. Our schools were overcrowded, and maybe half my class of more than 400 kids went to college. Cars had fins and a lot of chrome. We bought our clothes from the Sears Roebuck catalog or Penneys. On every July 4, one of the dads had to hide in his basement because the fireworks freaked him out. WWII was very bad for him.

Both my parents were great readers and believed that the more education you could get, the happier you'd be. Our house was full of dark Russian novels, political philosophy and history books, and I read it all. My mom helped start the community colleges in Washington state, and served on the system's first board. She campaigned for clean water and voting rights, all while keeping my brothers and me in chocolate chip cookies for after-school treats. My dad said he'd pay for any college we could get into.

When the time came, my parents waved me off from Seattle's King Street Station [finished in 1906, topped by a 242-foot clock tower designed to mimic the San Marco campanile in Venice] for the four-day train journey to Bryn Mawr College, outside Philadelphia. Off I chugged, ever eastward, with a couple of suitcases and a grocery bag of peanut butter sandwiches and oranges.

I majored in political science. By 1967, my junior year, I concluded that America was too flawed for electoral politics to fix. I organized a 14-day orange juice-only fast. [I lost 10 pounds.] I volunteered in a Tom Hayden project to collect information from people in Philadelphia's Black ghetto about their greedy landlords, broken plumbing, daily insults and fears, their lack of a decent neighborhood grocery store. Folks were patient and kind enough to let me in the door—I'm sure I did nothing to help them, but what they taught me was priceless. I edited the college paper and wrote desperate articles about racism. I co-founded our college's chapter of SDS with the neighboring all-men's college, Haverford.

I sold antiwar buttons to dozens of sympathetic faculty. The dean, however, was not amused. "Why would you do such a thing?" she asked.

"Because I need the money."

"Well, Kit" [*portentous pause*], "would you do *anything for money*?" As if I were selling my body, or perhaps the plans for nuclear warheads.

For my senior yearbook picture, I turned in a photo of me at a huge antiwar demonstration in New York—one small person in an SDS crowd. I am wearing a plaid cotton dress and have a ribbon in my ponytail. For my uplifting senior year quote, I paraphrased Mao: "As long as there are people, every kind of miracle is possible."

Rather than get married or go to graduate school, which the vast majority of Bryn Mawr graduates did, I high-tailed it to the SDS National Office in Chicago with my boyfriend. We wrote and published SDS's national weekly newspaper. The next summer—after Chicago's hot and dangerous 1968—about a dozen of us SDSers went to Cuba to meet representatives of the South Vietnamese resistance and the North Vietnamese army. We assembled at JFK airport in New York were given tickets to Havana via Mexico City. When we transferred to our Air Cubana flight in Mexico, the CIA was there on the tarmac, photographing us. My FBI file includes a few pages of my CIA file commemorating this international itinerary.

The Vietnamese guerrilla delegation, some of whom had traveled for two months to reach Havana for this summit, truly overestimated the revolutionary potential of American kids. We desperately wanted to live up to their example, believing we could successfully paste rural developing-world jungle warfare tactics onto the streets of Chicago, New York, Washington, D.C.

I sat next to one of the Vietnamese women on a bus one day as the Cubans toured us around their farmlands and cattle ranches. We passed a hayfield bordered by multiple strings of barbed-wire fencing. Pointing to the wire, the woman turned to me and said in quiet, halting English, "America has put a lot of that in Vietnam."

What was left of my Seattle middle-class future wavered like haze on the tarmac.

Back in the U.S.A., all fired up, we plotted the most violent multiday antiwar rampage we could imagine. Four days in October 1969. Chicago. We called it the "Days of Rage." We worked for months to organize thousands of kids to come kick ass on Chicago's mean streets. But we wouldn't just march. Every day we would run madly through the city's high-end retail and financial centers, break windows, start fires, do stuff that would show how tough we were. Our motto was "Bring the War Home!"

Oddly enough, very few kids were interested in going to jail that October. Instead of thousands, we had maybe 400. Almost all of us, including me, ended up in Cook County jail. My liberal dad was not happy and refused to bail me out. He said I was a fanatic. For us, jail proved more dumb and uncomfortable than scary. All of us women were on the

pill, which was immediately confiscated. Cold turkey, we all started to menstruate at once, messing up the jail matrons' work and supply cabinet.

After I left that Oakland protest in 1973, no longer planning to die an urban guerrilla, I read my way through my pregnancy. I kept reading right through my first four years of motherhood, nursing school, my return to Seattle and a clinical position at Seattle Children's Hospital.

History introduced me to a Seattle I hadn't known. The largest city in the distant upper-left-hand corner of the United States was not always the wealthy and worldly purveyor of software, airplanes, caffeine, philanthropy, grunge and online retail experience that it is today. On the contrary, in the early 1900s, Seattle was a gritty, wide-open, muddy, shack-filled seaport of several hundred thousand people who happily welcomed gamblers, prostitutes and bootleggers, along with the sailors, lumberjacks, fish and fruit packers, shipbuilders and haulers who enjoyed such diversions. Somehow, though, a thread connected those days to my days; it ran through the lives of women whose lives and convictions were a familiar echo of mine.

On a summer afternoon in 1913, Seattleite Annie Miller was giving a soapbox speech to a small crowd of townsfolk. She stood on red-bricked Washington Street in Pioneer Square, the very site where, barely 60 years earlier, the first white settlers had chopped down trees and shoved aside the Indigenous peoples. Mrs. Miller spoke forcefully in opposition to the U.S. entering what we now call World War I. The inevitable sidewalk scuffle broke out in Mrs. Miller's audience, between pro-war and antiwar listeners. *The Seattle Times*, owned by the archconservative Alden Blethen [the paper is still majority-owned by the Blethen family], described the event as a major street brawl. The article gleefully describes bloody battles between "a gang of red flag worshippers and anarchists" and soldiers and sailors "who had dared protest against the insults heaped on the American flag."

The next day, fueled by the paper's vitriol, mobs of men marched through Seattle streets. *The Times* headline read, "Anarchy in Seattle Stamped Out When Sailors Get Busy," and described a mob "fired with patriotic enthusiasm and armed only with small American flags" who, unimpeded by police, ransacked and burned newsstands and offices of socialist and anarchist groups.

Four years later, the war in full force, Louise Olivereau, a young woman who worked in one of those offices, faced sedition charges for urging draftees to think about the purposes and consequences of war and consider becoming conscientious objectors. She defended herself at trial, arguing that the U.S. was "at the mercy of war-mad fanatics" and that "our dearest ideals of freedom and human dignity [are being] dragged through the blood and dust of a war for financial profit." She was convicted and imprisoned.

I wish I'd been at her trial, sitting up front with a young woman journalist named Anna Louise Strong, who'd been a student at my college 50 years before me. Strong shared Olivereau's pacifism and political fire; she'd also covered the 1916 Everett Massacre, when five striking unarmed lumbermen were shot to death and dozens more injured by police and vigilantes in a small town just north of Seattle. She then came into her own as an active participant in the 1919 Seattle General Strike. This nearly weeklong strike is often studied today for its uniqueness, its lack of violence and its solidarity across unions and trade groups. Strikers took over all city functions: garbage collection, social services, maintenance of order. Strong wrote a fiery yet humble editorial saying: "We are undertaking the most tremendous move ever taken by LABOR in this country, a move which will lead NO ONE KNOWS WHERE!"

In the 1912 mayoral election, the Socialist candidate almost won. Seattle and Washington state women gained the right to vote a decade before the U.S. Constitution's 19th Amendment. One of our early newspapers was the first daily labor newspaper in the country. In 1926, Seattle became the first large American city to elect a woman mayor. Of course there's always opposition—judges, landowners, shop owners, manufacturers, newspaper owners, politicians, all fighting to keep their disproportionately luxurious share of the economic pie. And in a notably white corner of the country, Black, Indigenous, Asian and Hispanic communities had different, often more difficult, battles to fight. But it's now easy to trace yesterday's struggles, and impossible not to notice how they foreshadow today's. The stories of these women helped me understand where my Seattle came from, and why I'm happy that it's still my hometown.

I specialized in pediatric oncology at Seattle Children's Hospital, got married and had another daughter. The youngest was in high school in 1999, when the biggest street protests in Seattle since the Vietnam War erupted to protest the work of the World Trade Organization. She wanted to be part of it. OK, but I was going with her. Who better than me to show her the ropes? Protests can be, in part, a challenging puzzle: knowing when to go forward, when to retreat, the routes through the alleys and back streets, how to read the tactical intentions of the police. You can predict their behavior by their dress, the length of their batons, their guns, the presence or absence of shields and backup vehicles. There's a dangerous, adrenaline-fueled lure to it all.

Or protest can be something very different from all of that. In June 2020, my daughter, her husband and I joined a very diverse, 60,000-strong, silent Black Lives Matter march against police brutality and systemic racism. We walked almost 2 miles between two parks in a working-class Seattle neighborhood. Almost everyone in masks, trying to maintain the social distancing demanded of a pandemic-stricken world. In the pouring rain. Not a cop to be seen.

Meanwhile, a self-declared autonomous zone, a distant but distinct echo of the 1919 Seattle General Strike, arose in another part of town, with medical services, trash pickup, vegetable gardens and teach-ins about structural and personal racism, white privilege and police brutality. The mayor [again, a woman] promised to reform the police department. President Trump fumed on Twitter about terrorists in Seattle, and Fox News ran digitally altered photos to show burning buildings, broken windows and armed protesters. It was like a mashup of the 19th and 20th centuries, all in one.

I'm writing this just days after that march, just weeks after the murder of George Floyd in Minneapolis touched off the most profound American protest movement since those late '60s and early '70s days. The drumbeat to identify and end structural racism is only growing stronger here. The phenomenal impact of a silent march spoke volumes. It shouted the seriousness of the problem, the commitment of the marchers. As some of the marchers' signs read, it's all about equality, not revenge.

For my part, instead of ending up dead on some barricade by now, I'm just bushwhacking my way along. My maps are creased and stained, scrawled over with marginal updates. But the same better horizon is still out there and well worth the journey. Like the city itself. Anna Louise Strong might say: We are headed, no one knows where.

KIT BAKKE is a Seattle native. Her most recent book is *Protest on Trial: The Seattle 7 Conspiracy*. She has one husband, two daughters, two sons-in-law and two grandchildren.

SEATTLE, 1974

Written by **CHARLES D'AMBROSIO**

THE INITIAL SALVOS in my hankering to expatriate took the predictable route of firing snobby potshots at the local icons of culture, at Ivar with his hokey ukulele and Stan Boreson and Dick Balch with his ten-pound sledge bashing cars and laughing like a maniac all through the late night, etc. [Actually I thought DB was cool and so did a good many of my friends. He had the crude sinister good looks of a porn star and once merited an admiring squib in *Time*. In his cheap improvised commercials—interrupting roller derby and the antics of Joanie Weston the Blonde Amazon—he'd beat brand new cars with a hammer, so to me he always seemed superior to circumstance—our old cars just got beat to hell by life, whereas Dick Balch went out on the attack. It was a period when a lot of us hero-worshipped people who destroyed things and even now I wonder where DB's gone and half hope he'll come back and smash more stuff.]

Anyone born in geographical exile, anyone from the provinces, anyone for whom the movements of culture feel rumored, anyone like this grows up anxiously aware that all the innovative and vital events in the world happen Back East, like way back, like probably France, but before expatriation can be accomplished in fact it is rehearsed and performed in the head. You make yourself clever and scoffing, ironic, deracinated, cold and quick to despise. You import your enthusiasms from the past, other languages, traditions. You make the voyage first in the aisles of bookstores and libraries, in your feckless dreams. The books you love best feature people who ditched their homes in the hinterlands for scenes of richer glory. Pretty soon the word *Paris* takes on a numinous quality and you know you won't be silent forever. Someday you'll leave.

Meanwhile, the only city I really knew was a dump worse than anything Julius Pierpont Patches [local TV clown] ever dreamed of, sunk in depression and completely off the cultural map, no matter what outlandish claims local boosters made for the region. And they made many. In a highly cherished book of mine [*You Can't Eat Mount Rainier!*, by William Speidel Jr., Bob Cram illustrator, copyright 1955] I read "What with the city's leading professional men, artists, writers, world travelers and visiting VIP's always dropping into the place, [Ivar's] has become the spot where clams and culture meet." Huh? Artists? Writers? To explain, Ivar's is a local seafood restaurant and Ivar himself was a failed folk singer in the tradition of the Weavers. Back then there was an abundance of clams and a paucity of culture, but even more than this disparity, I'd somehow arranged it in my head that clams, salmon, steelhead and geoducks were actually antithetical to and the sworn enemies of culture. No one wrote about them, is what I probably meant. Perhaps clams and culture met, once, in 1955, but then of course 1955 stubbornly persisted in Seattle until like 1980, and in between time you felt stuck mostly with mollusks. The culture side of the equation was most prominently represented by a handful of aging rear-guard cornballs. Like Ivar himself.

If you were a certain type, and I was, you first had to dismantle the local scene's paltry offerings and then build up in its place a personal pantheon remote from the very notion that clams and culture really ever do meet, anywhere, at a time when, all arrogant and hostile and a budding prig, you believed culture was the proprietary right of a few Parisians. That an old warbly-voiced yokel like Ivar might pass for culture, or that "Here Come the Brides" might signify to the world your sense of place, seemed a horror, an embarrassment. I went incognito, I developed alibis. For starters I took to wearing a black Basque beret and became otherwise ludicrously francophile in my tastes. Mostly, however, I couldn't find solid purchase for my *snobisme*. Not that I didn't try. I'd have liked to be some old hincty Henry James but couldn't really sustain it.

Still, you badly wanted things delocalized, just a little. Even if you had to do it first just in your head, with issueless irony. You looked about. With a skeptical eye you sized up the offerings. You wondered, for instance, why it was that suddenly in Seattle there was an aesthetic love of statues. You wondered, what is it with all these replicas of people around the region? A brass Ivar and his brass seagulls, some apparently homeless people [brass] in the courtyard of the Sedgewick James Bldg. [as if a real, non-brass loiterer could actually rest awhile on those benches unmolested], and then, last, least, a hideous band of five or six citizens [cement] waiting for the bus in Fremont. Like a bunch of gargoyles walked off their ancient job guttering rain, they've been waiting for the bus twenty or thirty years now. If you've lived here long enough [like a week] you know the rain of today is the rain of tomorrow and the rain of a million years ago and if you stand in that eternal rain long enough and often enough the experience rubs it in your face. I've stood in the rain and waited for buses or whatever and it wasn't a joke, not that I understood, at least. You're standing there, you're buzzed, you're bored, you're waiting, you don't have a schedule, the rain's pounding around your head like nuthouse jibberjabber, and from this

TODAY I GO IN SEARCH OF AN OLDER CITY, A SILENT CITY. EARLY IN THE MORNING THE PAINTED SIGNS DOWN-TOWN SEEM TO RISE AWAY FROM THE BRICK IN A KIND OF LAYERED PENTIMENTO.

incessant and everlasting misery someone else works up an instance of passing cleverness, then casts it in concrete for all time?

Those stone citizens, silent and forever waiting, are like my nightmare.

I badly wanted to escape my unwritten city for a time and place already developed by words, for Paris or London or Berlin and a particular epoch as it existed in books. I wanted Culture, the upper case sort. Books fit my minimum-wage budget and afforded the cheapest access. Fifty cents bought admission to the best. I purchased most of my early novels and poems from a woman who, I recall, only had one leg. Later there was Elliott Bay Books, which offered both a bookstore and a brick walled garret in the basement. You could loiter without having to skulk. You could bring your empty cup to the register and ask for refills. And you could read. Those books, more than any plane ticket, offered a way out. Admittedly it was a lonely prescription, an Rx that might better have been replaced by a 100 mg of whatever tricyclate was cutting edge back in the Seventies. But who knew about such things? Instead I'd hide out in basement of Elliott Bay or in the top floor of the Athenian and in my sporadic blue notebooks track a reading list—Joyce, Pound, Eliot et al.—that was really little more than a syllabus for a course on exile.

You could probably dismiss this as one of those charming agonies of late adolescence, but let me suggest that it's also a logical first step in developing an aesthetic, a reach toward historical beauty, the desire to join yourself to what's already been appreciated and admired. You want to find yourself in the flow of time, miraculously relieved of your irrelevance. For reasons both sensible and suspect folks today are uneasy with the idea of a tradition, but the intellectual luxury of this stance wasn't available to me, and I saw the pursuit of historical beauty, the yearning for those higher essences other people had staked their lives on, as the hope for some kind of voice, a chance to join the chorus. I was mad for relevance, connection, some hint that I was not alone. I started scribbling in notebooks in part just so I'd have an excuse, a reason for sitting where I sat, an alibi for being by myself.

Seattle in the Seventies was the nadir of just everything. A UW prof of mine, a yam-faced veteran of SDS, inelegantly labeled us the phlegmatic generation. The word *apathy* got used an awful lot. I quite sincerely believe Karen Ann Quinlan was the decade's sex symbol. Seeking an alchemic dullness in quaaludes and alcohol she actually found apotheosis in a coma, that's what made her so sexy [i.e. compelling] and symbolic to me. I'm not trying to be ironic or waggish here. Objects restore a measure of silence to the world, and she was, for those ten wordless years, an object. Her speechless plight seemed resonant, Delphic. The reason I remember her as such an emblematic figure is her coma coincided with my own incognizant youth. The Seattle of that time had a distinctly comalike aspect and at night seemed to contain in its great sleepy volume precisely one of everything, one dog abarking, one car acranking, one door aslamming etc, and then an extravagant, unnecessary amount of nothing. Beaucoup nothing. The kind of expansive, hardly differentiated, foggy and final nothing you imagine a coma induces. I read the silence as a kind of Nordic parsimony. An act of middle-class thrift. A soporific seeded into the clouds. All the decent dull blockheads were asleep, and you could no more wake them to vivid life than you could KAQ. Being alone at night in Seattle began to seem horrifying, there was just so much nothing and so little of me.

You know how the story goes—I went away, I came back, blah blah. I now see the personal element in all this, the comic note, and I also realize the high European graft doesn't readily take to all American subjects. The predominant mental outlook of people I grew up with depended largely on a gargantuan isolation. When I finally went away I was always careful to tell people I was from Seattle, Washington, afraid they wouldn't know where the city was, which suggests the isolation of the place was permanently lodged in me. Finding myself at last in the warm heart of culture, in New York or Paris or even LA, I returned, like some kind of revanchist, to the cold silent topography I knew best, the landscape of my hurt soul. I first read Raymond Carver because in paging through his second collection at a bookstore I noticed a familiar place name—Wenatchee—and latched on to the work solely based on that simple recognition. Ditto Ken Kesey. And then there was the discovery of Richard Hugo, a great epic namer, who beautifully described himself as "a wrong thing in a right world," and noted the oppressive quiet of the city the way I had, so that it seemed we were brothers, and offered to me a liberating emblem far better suited to my ambitions as a writer than a girl in a coma. These are probably just the humdrum dilemmas any writer encounters, and that I should express any keen pain at the difficulty of finding a subject and a voice is, I realize, kind of carping and obnoxious. It comes with the territory, after all.

And yet it is still some form of familiar silence that I struggle against when I write, something essential about the isolation. As Graham Greene wrote: "At that age one may fall irrevocably in love with failure, and success of any kind loses half its savour before it is experienced." For me the city is still inarticulate and dark and a place I call home because I'm in thrall to failure and to silence—I have a fidelity to it, an allegiance, which presents a strange dislocation now that Seattle's become the Valhalla of so many people's seeking. The idea of it as a locus of economic and scenic and cultural hope baffles me. It a little bit shocks me to realize my nephew and nieces are growing up in a place considered desirable. That will be their idea, rightly. That wasn't my idea at all. Vaguely groping for a diluted tertiary memory, people used to say to me, I've heard it's nice out there, and I'd say, Seattle has a really high suicide rate [I was kind of an awkward conversationalist]. But really I didn't know if it was nice; it never occurred to me to wonder. I'd shyly shrug and mumble out of the conversation, saying I didn't know, it was home. Seattle does have a suicide rate a couple notches above the national average and so does my family and I guess that earns me the colors of some kind of native. I walk around, I try to check it out, this new world of hope and the good life, but in some part of my head it's forever 1974 and raining and I'm a kid and a man with a shopping cart full of kiped meat clatters down the sidewalk chased with sad enthusiasm by apron-wearing boxboys who are really full-grown men recently pink-slipped at Boeing and now scabbing part-time at Safeway.

Today I go in search of an older city, a silent city. Early in the morning the painted signs on the buildings downtown seem to rise away from the brick in a kind of layered pentimento. The light at that hour comes at a certain angle and is gentle and noticeably slower and words gradually emerge from the walls. *Your Credit Is Good. The Best In Raingear.* There is a place I can stand on Westlake Avenue and read the fading signs and recognize many of the names of people I grew up with. I've got my own people buried in the ground. I cross the Aurora Bridge and think special thoughts and know my brother's black wellingtons are buried in the shifting toxic silt at the bottom of Lake Union. That brother's alive, and I thank God for certain kinds of failure. New silences layer over the old. I hope this brief superficial essay hasn't simply circled around a peculiar woundedness. Folks double my age and older often run down a conversation tracking a vanishing world that will, with the passing of their memory, vanish entirely. This is something more than benign senescent forgetfulness. So be it. Nowadays I feel like an old timer in terms of estrangement. I don't know what determines meaning in the city any better than these old people with their attenuating memories. Probably traffic laws, the way we still agree to agree on the denotation of stop signs. I went away and in my absence other things have sprung up. Good things. It's a new place, but there's an old silence bothering me.

And now when I write I feel the silence pressuring the words just like the silence I felt as a kid, walking around town, with nowhere to go. It used to be I'd wander down the alley around the corner from the Yankee Peddler and see if Floyd the Flowerman was in his shack. FF sold flowers out of a homemade shack, a lean-to patched together out of realtor's sandwich boards and such and propped up against what's now a soap shop, and he was a big fan of police scanners, of the mysteries of other people's misfortunes as they cackled over the airwaves and received, at least briefly, a specific locus, a definite coordinate within the city. This oddball interest in fixing the detailed location of pain and disaster fascinated me. I'd say it prefigured the job of a writer, if the conceit weren't so obviously tidy. I can't now tell if Floyd was crazy. Probably he was just sixties jetsam, tossed overboard by the era and living like a kind of alley cat Brautigan "made lonely and strange by that Pacific Northwest of so many years ago, that dark rainy land ..." That wet black alley, and then the queer miracle of his white shack, those floodlit plaster buckets filled with red gladiolas, sunflowers, pink carnations, and then Floyd the hippie holdover tuning his scanner into instances of tragedy, dialing up meaning and its shifting vectors. One night when the bus just wouldn't come, Floyd and I walked in the rain down Stone Way to watch a house burn. He was very hepped up. The cold rain on our faces warmed to tear-temperature in the heat of the burning house. I wish time would collapse so I could be watching flames and ash rise from that house and also see my brother falling through the air below the bridge. Obscurely I know this is a wish that Time, like a god, might visit us all in our moment of need. But Floyd's gone and that brother's got a metal plate in his pelvis and walks a little funny and myself, I wander around at night, taking long walks to clear my head before sitting down in front of my typewriter, walking for an hour or two as all the new and desirable good floats before me like things in a dream, out of reach, and I peer through the windows of new restaurants and new shops and see all the new people but I don't go in, probably because I feel more in my element as the man who is out there standing in the rain or just passing by on his way home to write.

CHARLES D'AMBROSIO is the author of two collections of short stories, *The Point* and *The Dead Fish Museum*, and two essay collections, *Orphans* and *Loitering*. He's been the recipient of a Whiting Award and a Lannan Literary Fellowship, among other honors. He teaches fiction at the Iowa Writers' Workshop. An early version of this essay appeared in *The Stranger*; it is anthologized in *Loitering*.

INDEX

INDEX